TEACHING YOUR CHILD TO WRITE

TEACHING YOUR CHILD TO WRITE

How Parents Can Encourage
Writing Skills—for Success
in School, Work, and Life

CHERI FULLER

BERKLEY BOOKS, NEW YORK

This book is an original publication of The Berkley Publishing Group.

TEACHING YOUR CHILD TO WRITE

A Berkley Book / published by arrangement with
the author

PRINTING HISTORY
Berkley trade paperback edition / September 1997

The Putnam Berkley World Wide Web site address is http://www.berkley.com

ISBN: 0-425-15983-3

BERKLEY®
Berkley Books are published by The Berkley Publishing Group, a
member of Penguin Putnam Inc.,
200 Madison Avenue, New York, New York 10016.
BERKLEY and the "B" design
are trademarks belonging to Berkley Publishing Corporation.

PRINTED IN THE UNITED STATES OF AMERICA

10 9 8 7 6 5 4 3 2 1

Contents

Dear Parent ix

Chapter 1   Kids Who Write   1

Chapter 2   The Building Blocks: Foundations for Writing in the Early Years   11

Chapter 3   Providing a Writing Environment   21

Chapter 4   Growing up Writing: Ages, Stages, and Readiness to Write   30

Chapter 5   How Writers Write: Understanding the Writing Process   45

Chapter 6   Writing Letters for Fun, Friends, and Profit   60

Chapter 7   Write Away! Using E-mail to Boost Your Child's Writing Skills   75

Chapter 8   Across the Miles: Writing Family Newsletters and Neighborhood Newspapers   85

Chapter 9   Help, Mom! I've Got to Write a Book Report   92

Chapter 10   Creative Journal Keeping: The Best Practice for Developing Writers   102

Chapter 11	Story Writing Exercises	113
Chapter 12	Bookmaking Projects for Children	122
Chapter 13	Writing Family History Stories	136
Chapter 14	Fun with Words: Word Play for Every Age	144
Chapter 15	Poetry Writing: The Magic of the Written Word	155
Chapter 16	Helping Young Writers Break into Print	175
Appendix	A Grammar Guide	189
	Guidelines for Assessing Children's Writing	203
	Magazines That Publish Young Authors	208
ABC Book Ideas		213

Acknowledgments

This book represents a long journey of learning, teaching, being involved with young writers of all ages, and parenting our own three children for twenty-five years while passing on my love of writing. I wish I could personally thank each teacher I had throughout school that sparked my love of writing, but if you read this, know I am grateful.

Many thanks to Posy Lough for sharing her creative ideas on book report alternatives and blank book construction. I appreciate all the teachers I've worked with in classrooms as I directed Young Author's Workshops. Thanks to Vivian Nida and Kay Bishop, Janet Martin, Deborah Morris, and Beverly Murray for sharing your ideas and your writing experiences. Thank you, Jessica and Peggy Stewart for your assistance and encouragement! And especially two special teachers, Lu Rice and Marilee Hattendorf, who have an excitement about teaching writing I wish for every teacher in America—thanks for letting me write with your students and for your reading of and enthusiasm about this book.

Thanks to Dr. Judy Abbott for her insightful research on children's writing, and to Sally Rubottom, Melissa King, and Dr. Tim Campbell, Associate Professor at the University of Central Oklahoma, for their reading and input on the manuscript. And to the many home school parents and children in Oklahoma that I've had the opportunity of working with in writing workshops, I'm grateful.

To all the children and teens I've worked with through the years and especially those whose writing has been included in this book—I've learned much from you and been enriched by your writing and I thank you. Much appreciation goes to my own three children, Justin, Christopher, and Alison—you have been so much fun to write with and write to through the years; thanks for letting me use some of your childhood writings.

Many thanks to Denise Silvestro, my editor at Berkley, for her insights and editing skills on this project, and my agent Greg Johnson. And most of all, to my husband, Holmes, *thank you for everything,* especially the spaghetti dinners you fixed while I was working on this manuscript.

Dear Parent,

You've bought this book because you want to help your child become a stronger writer and thus achieve more in school and life. I commend you for participating in your child's education. Your child will benefit enormously from your involvement, support, and enthusiasm for writing and all the learning she does at school and home.

Writing is such an important skill for children to master, yet sometimes parents (and even teachers) avoid it because they are intimidated by grammar rules, don't feel they were good writers in school, or don't know how to teach writing. Take heart!

In these pages you are going to find many activities that will develop your child's love of writing—activities that are easy and fun. There are practical exercises on everything from writing personal experience stories to writing poems and book reports. You'll find special projects like how to create a family newsletter and how your child can keep a travel journal; projects that make use of E-mail and the Internet, and many fun and practical reasons to write letters. There are ideas for word play, storytelling, and treasure hunts for rainy days.

There are practical guidelines and exercises to help you instill good old-fashioned grammar skills, tips to smooth the writing process, and specific ways for you to nourish your child's creative spark. There's even a chapter on how to help your child break into print and get her best writing published.

To get the maximum use of *Teaching Your Child to Write*, read of the terrific benefits that children receive when they develop good writing skills in the first chapter, "Kids Who Write." Don't miss the foundations for writing in chapter 2, especially if your child is a preschooler or in the early years of school. Chapter 3 will help you gather materials for your child's writing center and you'll see all the ways home can become a fun place to write. In chapter 4, "Growing up Writing," you'll discover the writing skills that kids develop at certain ages and activities to match their skills. The remainder of the book provides fun activities for children of all ages. Pick a chapter with writing projects that will appeal to your child: If she loves poetry and word play, try "Fun with Words." If she's a natural-born storyteller, let her try her hand at creating a "scar" story in chapter 11.

The most important thing is to encourage your child to write regularly. This book offers many ways to do that, with activities that even the busiest families can fit in because they make writing a part of everyday life. For children, doing things together as a family makes happy memories, so I encourage you to do some of the writing activities with your child. Others can be done individually or with a friend. Your interest and involvement in your child's learning—and especially writing—is a great gift you'll both enjoy.

CHAPTER 1

Kids Who Write

*Writing, like life itself,
is a voyage of discovery.*
—Henry Miller

"RobotMan calculated the distance between his destination on Pluto and his current position circling the moon. The yellow alarm light flashed *Fuel Leak*! He scanned the projectathon and realized that an attempt to escape might leave him lost in space. From below, a laser missile fired another hole in his fuel tank. He glanced back at the warships gaining on him and thrust to full speed. He'd take his chance in space. . . . "

Fifth grader Andrew looked up from the latest science fiction story he'd written in his writer's notebook and glowed at the rapt attention of his family around the dinner table.

"Read some more!" his brother begged.

Sixteen-year-old Nick left a note for his mom: "I'm going to Braum's for ice cream with Nathan and will be back at 2:35. While I'm gone, please do these things: feed the dog, start dinner, and have fun! Love, Nick." (A play on all the notes she'd left listing chores *he* needed to do before leaving home!)

Five-year-old Katherine goes to her "office," the desk in her walk-in closet where she loves to write poetry and stories about animals, princesses, and the caterpillars she found in the yard.

These are children who've learned that writing is useful in everyday life, that it's worth their time, and that, in fact, it is fun. They aren't unusual or nerdy bookworms, but kids whose family life supports their emerging literacy and encourages their development as writers. Your child can learn to write well and love writing.

Why Write?

This is a book about building a love for writing and developing writing skills in our children. Whether you are a parent with a child in school and a desire to supplement her school writing, a parent educating your child at home, or a teacher wishing to enliven your students' writing program, this book is for you.

Why all this fuss about writing? Because writing is not just another subject. Writing means fully formulating your ideas and articulating and expressing them on paper. That's why writing affects your child's learning and achievement in every single subject. A good writer is a good thinker.

If your child becomes an effective writer, he will not only enjoy self-expression, but he'll learn to use writing to build friendships, express appreciation, and work with people. He'll also become more self-reliant in homework and have a more enjoyable learning experience from first grade through college. He'll be more successful in every subject and be able to convey his ideas on the hundreds of tests, reports, and assignments he'll face.

What's the Problem?

Research shows that many students have trouble organizing their thoughts coherently in writing. One study revealed that 80 percent of the 55,000 students tested could not write an adequate letter or a persuasive essay. Most of the children's writing lacked clarity, coherence, and organization.[1]

Another national writing assessment showed that 73 percent of fourth graders and 43 percent of eighth graders scored low on informative writing (such as reports on a news event after reading the facts). Half of the students surveyed said they would never write if it weren't for school assignments. Three-fourths of the students said an ability to write isn't necessary to get a job, and many couldn't properly fill out a job application. Only a third said writing is a good way to tell others your ideas.

When writing skills are lacking, a child may have great ideas but produce confusing compositions and get low test grades. When a student's thoughts come across in a garbled, often misspelled style, she gets labeled lazy or even lacking in intelligence. In junior high and high school she may just barely pass, but in college with more demands for research papers and essays and higher expectations, it only gets worse.

In response to these alarming studies, millions of dollars were invested to improve school writing programs. Many teachers were trained in better teaching techniques and new writing programs were piloted. Schools made efforts to have students write in subjects like science and history instead of just English class.

However, because of overcrowded classrooms, lack of funding, and already jam-packed curricula, many students still aren't doing much writing. Instead, they are assigned tasks that are easier to grade, such as multiple choice tests and worksheets instead of essay exams and compositions. And so, our children still can't write.

Educating Children at Home: Does Writing Take a Backseat?

If you are a home school parent, you may find that writing gets shoved aside in lieu of other activities in your curriculum. Perhaps the only writing your child regularly does is filling in blanks in

[1] National Assessment of Educational Progress, 1986.

workbooks. Unfortunately, no one I've ever known became a better writer by filling workbook blanks with words. Improved writing comes through lots of meaningful writing experiences.

Why is it that although home schooling is an ideal environment for children to grow into good writers, many don't write? As I've talked with parents about this problem, some of the responses are: "I don't know how to critique it or grade it when it's just a story." Another mom said, "I'm a poor writer because I never had a teacher who had us do creative writing or even just to write regularly. I feel very inadequate myself as a writer so I don't know how to help or encourage my kids' writing." Finally, a parent summed it up: "A lot of us feel we have a mental block in writing and lack a good background."

Unless you are a writer yourself or had a rich school experience of writing, you may identify with these parents' frustration with teaching writing. That's why this book will be helpful. No matter what your background or lack of experience in writing, you will discover ways to improve your child's language skills and assess her writing. In addition, you will be equipped to make writing a regular part of your everyday family lifestyle and learning and thus help your children become lifelong writers.

Helping Kids Write: The Benefits

One of the bright spots of all the research in the past two decades has been the finding that when kids are encouraged to share their writing with enthusiastic parents and friends, they become better writers. A youngster who writes at home learns to value writing and puts more effort into it. He becomes more proficient in writing and has a head start in every school task. Those benefits continue throughout life.

There are over thirty million jobs today in which people use writing to convey and transfer information as part of their daily work: engineers write reports, account executives write marketing proposals, lawyers write briefs, social workers write case studies. There are memos to compose, advertising copy to create, job résumés, and political campaign writing. There is a need for good writing in newspapers, television and movie scripts, magazines and professional journals, financial forms, police reports, business letters, and instructions on how to use products.

Because we are an information-oriented world, our culture depends on a precise and effective use of spoken and written language. The young person who can communicate effectively in writing and speech will be the adult who can rise to the top of any field and impact his profession and community.

Putting the Ball in Their Hands

Why should *you* encourage your child's writing? Because you have a profound influence on the development of writing, reading, listening, and thinking skills in your children.

Parents tend to encourage and give opportunity for their kids to develop in the areas of their own interests. If you love sports, for example, you probably put a ball in your baby's hands at an early age and taught him how to bounce, handle, and kick it. You may have signed your four-year-old up for a pee-wee soccer team. If you're an artist, you probably have a table somewhere in the house with clay, paint, and other art materials for your child to use. A physicist dad I know helped his nine-year-old son build a model of a working dam just because they'd seen a picture in the encyclopedia and his son wanted to try it. It was no big deal to him, just a little project they both enjoyed.

When that kind of influence happens, as long as the parent doesn't push or force the activity, the child often develops an aptitude and interest in the sport or hobby. We see this parental impact in the area of music. Research on professional musicians shows that the most common factor in their experience is that their parents sang a lot at home and had instruments around the house, not that they were enrolled in formal private music lessons at age three or five.

In our family's case, since I'd been a lifelong writer of letters and poems, my children were surrounded by words. They still chuckle about the long lists I'd leave when I had to be gone for the afternoon:

lists of chores to be accomplished, suggested fun activities, and even a few don'ts. Besides leaving daily notes of encouragement or reminders on yellow sticky paper and reading to them a great deal, I occasionally wrote a poem and gave it as a gift on a special occasion. They saw me writing in my journal and writing letters. Often, we played word games while driving to school or on car trips. When they began their own writing, I saved each year's creations in a separate file folder and displayed their poems and stories taped to the refrigerator or even framed and hung on the wall.

The result? Although our children are quite different in aptitude, each has become an extremely competent writer. Chris, twenty-two, a premed student, is very science-oriented, yet his ability to answer essay questions and do college writing has helped him excel in physics and chemistry in addition to humanities, philosophy, and language courses. Recently, Chris has begun writing a philosophy book for college students. Justin, twenty-five, majored in English and business law in college and uses writing in his field of work, advertising, as he writes marketing proposals, numerous letters, and radio commercial scripts for clients. He has a plot outline for a novel he plans to write someday.

Our daughter, Alison, twenty, is a fluent, creative writer, although art and music are her forte. She writes songs and is able to express her deepest feelings and ideas on paper when she can't talk about them. Both Alison and Justin have had poems published in national youth magazines.

You don't have to be a professional writer to encourage your children's writing skills. I'll pass along my best secrets and offer you dozens of easy ways you can become a writing family. Sooner than you think you'll be on your way to encouraging your children's developing skills, and maybe you'll find a new enjoyment in writing yourself.

Families That Write at Home

Dr. Judy Abbott, assistant professor of education at West Virginia University, did a fascinating doctoral dissertation that underscores the importance of parents encouraging children to write at home. Her research involved an in-depth study of fifth grade students termed "avid writers," who choose to write on their own. The young people she found who engaged in "self-sponsored writing" were skillful language users who had more facility and interest in writing than their peers. Not award-winning writers, but kids with a variety of interests, among them writing. Through hundreds of hours of observation in their homes and during interviews, Abbott examined what factors in their family supported their writing, and her findings were important:

• These young writers had a lot of adult interaction in their young life and thus began their oral language either early or at the normal developmental time. With much talking and conversation at home, they took on more adult patterns of language than other children and seemed to have an understanding and facility with language that helped immensely when they began to take on written language through reading and writing.

• The people around the children treated their first writing attempts as real writing and took it seriously, trying to decipher what they had written and have the child read it to them. They weren't told, "Oh, you're just doing pretend writing." Even when using invented spelling, their early writing was treated as real language.

• In the children's lives, there was at least one adult instrumental in interacting with them and their writing who took time to read aloud, talk about school issues, and encourage them to express themselves by casually suggesting things like, "That's such a good story you've told me; maybe you ought to write that down," or showing interest in their work: "Can I see what you've been writing?" They suggested practical writing like list-making (making a birthday list or a list of friends to invite over during the summer) and wrote notes to their children at home.

• Parents made time for these kids to write and create on a regular basis. The children had some free, unscheduled time to pursue their own interests and their parents provided instruments and resources, such as markers, pens, paper, and a computer to facilitate their writing. For instance, one mother, knowing her son had a hard time falling asleep, gave him extra time at night when lights would otherwise be out to read or write at his desk and jot down ideas as they came to him, which helped him relax.

• Each of the young writers had encountered a teacher somewhere in his or her school experiences who had acknowledged and supported their interest in writing, allowing them to choose topics to write on and releasing them from requirements when they showed competency so they could pursue the form of writing they were most interested in.

This study underscores how important adults are in facilitating a child's love of language, especially writing, as a lifelong skill. It also shows that the more we can talk to children about real issues and things that interest them, the more we encourage them to express their curiosity and write down their ideas, the better we will enrich their learning.

In addition, we can value all forms of writing. The youngsters Abbott interviewed did diverse writing: they wrote journals, stories, poetry, and took assignments the teacher had given and used them as a springboard to another form. They made menus, posters, and flyers for art shows or play events. They enjoyed making lists and planning a party on paper. They created comic books, business plans for a fictitious corporation, and fantasy tales. With all of their efforts, they got positive feedback from adults that these were worthwhile writing pursuits.

"We dismiss so much of what we as adults and children write because it's not a traditional or literary form like a story or poem," says Abbott. "Actually, most of us are writing all the time in work-related pursuits or at home." We're writing lists, letters, E-mails, newsletters, daily journals, and calendars, all of which require the same processes as literary-based writing. If we encourage kids to do all these kinds of writing, fewer of them will be reluctant to write. Most of all, we need to let our children observe us writing at home.

The more you write at home and let your kids see you, the more they'll understand that writing has value. They will realize that writing is a worthwhile way to spend time and be more inclined to do it themselves. They can discover that writing is as much fun as playing video games, building with Legos, drawing, or playing an instrument. When they see you write a letter to the editor of your local paper, write a marketing proposal for your job, or revise a letter to the school principal, they see real reasons for writing, and this provides a great background for their own writing and learning.

There are many ways to encourage children's writing. This book will offer not only many writing projects and ideas to get your child started, but ways to respond to kids' writing that encourages rather than discourages their efforts. When they write, they need our praise and affirmation, not criticism. They need to know that we value their poems and stories because we enjoy reading them, share them with others, and treasure them. Someone said that the greatest need children have besides love is appreciation. When we appreciate and enjoy their writing, their interest and skills begin to bloom.

This book will help you become a writing family, where you set the stage for learning, where you model an enjoyment of writing, and where you provide lots of reasons, resources, and encouragement for your child to write. If you are a home school parent, you will find much more than a year's worth of material to teach your children writing: projects like creating a book, scar stories, word play, poetry, and family newsletters. You'll also discover ways to supplement the writing your child does at school, how to write on the go when you take family trips, how to use the computer and E-mail to improve your child's communication skills, how to help your child learn to edit his writing, and much more. In the process, you'll be encouraging your child to become a lifelong writer who is more successful in every subject and equipped to communicate in his or her career and life. Let's write!

Exercises

1. Take a survey of your family at the dinner table. Ask each person how he uses writing in his daily life, job, or relationships, and

make a list of what different kinds of writing you do. Share with your child how writing helps you work with and communicate with people.

2. The next time your child writes something and shares it with you, post it on the refrigerator.

3. Write a grocery list together before going to the store.

4. If you or anyone in the family has ever written anything that has been published, show it to your child. It could be a self-published cookbook a relative gave for Christmas, an article published in a professional, trade, or vocational journal, memoirs of your grandfather, your own diary from teenage years, or something you wrote that appeared in the high school newspaper.

CHAPTER 2

The Building Blocks: Foundations for Writing in the Early Years

*Childhood's learning is made up of moments.
It isn't steady. It's a pulse . . . I live in
gratitude to my parents for initiating me—and
as early as I begged for it, without keeping me
waiting—into knowledge of the word,
into reading . . .*
—Eudora Welty

You pick your baby up and walk around the room, pointing out "doggy," "window," and other words. Neurons from his ears start making connections to the auditory cortex. You hold your infant up to see the bright decorations on the Christmas tree. An electrical connection is made from his retina to his brain's visual cortex. All the words, sights, and sounds that a child hears and experiences, even in the first months of life, begin forming a "perceptual map, the basic circuitry of language." [1] Thus, you play a key role in your child's language development, and your home is your child's first, most important literate environment.

New research shows that the early experiences of childhood program the brain's circuits, somewhat like a programmer wires the circuits of a computer (except the brain is infinitely more complex and has more potential than the most sophisticated computer). Each skill—math, music, logic, emotion, and most important for our topic,

[1] Sharon Begley, "Your Child's Brain," *Newsweek*, February 19, 1996, p.55.

language—has a critical period for learning when the gates of the mind are wide open and malleable.

This learning window or readiness for learning language extends from birth to ten years of age. During these vital years, the foundation is built for the reading, writing, speaking, and thinking abilities your child will draw from for the rest of his life. The first two years are so important that researchers have confirmed that the reason the Head Start students' progress is short-lived is that the intensive instruction begins too late to actually rewire the brain and make up for what the child missed in the first two critical years.[2]

Home: Where Language Learning Begins

What does this information mean for you as a parent? That language learning begins at home and that you play a key role in your child's language development. The more language experiences a child has and the more words a child hears between birth and age two, the larger her vocabulary will grow and the better her capacity for learning. For example, infants whose mothers spoke to them a lot during their first year knew 131 more words at twenty months than did babies of less talkative, less involved mothers. By twenty-four months old, the toddlers of talkative moms knew 295 more words. Hearing the sound of words builds up circuitry in the brain that then can absorb more words.[3] And the more proficient a child is in spoken language, the more successful she will be at reading written language and expressing her own understanding of things in writing because the communication skills of oral language, reading, and writing are interrelated.

So the first building blocks for your child's literacy are vital. Here are some first steps to build a strong foundation for writing in the early years:

Talk—a lot. From birth, talk to your child lovingly and gently, but don't use baby talk. Talk with your child while strolling through the

[2] Sharon Begley, "Your Child's Brain," *Newsweek*, February 19, 1996, p. 56.
[3] Sharon Begley, "Your Child's Brain," *Newsweek*, February 19, 1996, p. 57.

neighborhood, swinging and playing at the park, folding clothes, or cooking a meal in the kitchen. When you show your child the birds flying by the window, explain what they are doing. Use the correct names for things.

Talk to her about where you're going as you go about doing errands in the car together. Talk about the nutritious food you're feeding her at lunchtime: "Here are three grapes for you—one, two, three. This is your juice." Speak soothing words as you ready her for bedtime. Point to and label objects as you push your child down the colorful aisles in the grocery cart. Be specific with your language so your child will hear and clearly understand words for objects and actions. For example, instead of saying "Bring your things here, please," you might say "Please bring me your socks and shoes and we'll put them on and go outside!" Discuss what you just saw on television and what you're going to do tomorrow, what your child is playing with and curious about. Conversations about people, events, and experiences in the child's day-to-day life are important links in language learning.

Once your child is saying words and sentences, converse intelligently with her, and enjoy engaging in daily dialogue together. Children's listening vocabulary (words they hear and understand the meaning of) is always ahead of their speaking vocabulary.

The better children are at using spoken language (i.e., both listening and talking), research shows, the more successfully they will learn to read and write and the better they will do on aptitude and achievement tests in high school.[4]

Although conversation is an important building block in the development of children's literacy, most parents don't maximize the powerful opportunities to talk with their children. According to the U.S. Department of Education, American mothers spend only eight to fifteen minutes a day talking or explaining to their children, and fathers spend even less. But when parents do take the time to talk with their

[4] *What Works: Research About Teaching and Learning*, U.S. Department of Education, 1986, p. 15.

kids a lot, the results are positive. Sally, a mother of preschoolers, says she uses her normal vocabulary and explains things in as much detail as she can to answer their questions in order to provide her daughters with a great deal of verbal input. She encourages them to use words that describe what they see, smell, feel, hear, and taste. She finds that her children begin to use the new words in their own sentences and sees their verbal ability grow by leaps and bounds.

When your child begins to understand words enough to respond to them with action, give practice following directions and encourage listening skills. Even with toddlers and preschoolers, you can start with one simple request like, "Please bring your toy to Mommy." You can eventually add a second request: "Would you please bring Mom her boots and hat?" Be sure to thank your child and affirm her efforts at helping. This simple activity will foster good listening skills, which helps usher your child into the wonderful world of language.

Play games and sing songs with finger play. Songs with repetition and finger movements that go with the words, such as "Old MacDonald Had a Farm," "Where is Thumbkin?" and "I'm a Little Teapot," are a wonderful way to keep young children's attention and expand their language. Finger play songs are good time-fillers when waiting with restless little ones in the doctor's or dentist's office. As they grow, they can advance to games like Simon Says and I Spy and board games.

Limit television watching. The infant, toddler, and preschool years are too important to spend them in the passive pastime of watching television. Preschoolers should be allowed to watch no more than one hour of television a day; less is even better. If your child is in day care, be sure you know how much television viewing (including video movies) is included in his daily schedule.

According to experts such as Marie Winn, author of *The Plug-In Drug,* although the quality of programming is important, it's the quantity of television watching that is at issue. Since television is a nonverbal, primarily visual activity, it is never an adequate substitute for real-life language opportunities. "The greater the children's verbal opportunities, the greater the likelihood that their language will grow in complexity and rational, verbal thinking abilities will sharpen," says Winn. "The more they watch TV and thus the fewer the opportunities, on the other hand, the greater the likelihood that certain linguistic areas will remain undeveloped or underdeveloped as critical time periods come and go." [5]

When you do watch a television program together, discuss it with your child and ask questions like, "What do you think the character is going to do now?" or "Why did you like that show?"

Answer your child's questions enthusiastically. Young children ask myriad questions: Why do we have feet instead of wheels? Why does the cat have whiskers? Why is that green worm fuzzy?—and so many more! Their curiosity, the desire to know why, know how, and know more is built in from birth. Although their persistent questions may cause us occasional frustration (especially if you're trying to dress your child to get somewhere on time and he keeps asking questions), if we look at the benefits of questioning, it's worth the effort to respond positively.

Asking questions and hearing answers gives a child the chance to review what he just heard or saw, to get more information, to build vocabulary, to learn about the world around him, and to experience how language functions.

Questioning is so important that if stamped out, enthusiasm and motivation for learning dies. Conversely, if you keep the light of curiosity alive, you are fanning the flame of your child's whole desire to learn, read, write, wonder, and discover. Here are some ways to help your child know it pays to wonder and question.

• Listen to discover what your child is really thinking. Give her time to explain what she already knows and what she wants to know about a subject, and then build on what she already knows when you respond.

• Answer thoroughly, but avoid technical language.

• Help your child think about the question and ponder creatively about the answer. If he wants you to fit two boxes together, for

---

[5]Marie Winn, *The Plug-In Drug: Television, Children, and the Family*, NY: Viking Penguin Inc., 1985, p. 54.

instance, you could ask, "I wonder how these two boxes fit together? Let's see . . ." You don't have to give all the answers, but help your child deduce possible solutions.

Growing Young Readers

The next vital component of family literacy is developing a love for and skill in reading at home. A good foundation in reading is the cornerstone to helping children become better writers and learners. Conversely, every child who can't read has some problems in expressing himself through writing. When they read regularly, kids' knowledge of sentence structure, vocabulary, and grammar are all being painlessly reinforced. As they become better readers, their skills in both oral and written communication grow.

School is an important component of literacy development, but classroom experience can only build on the language skills that the child has already begun developing at home, so the first place for reading to be a priority is in the family.

Think of all the moments you have and language resources available in your home during the first few years as the soil of your child's garden of literacy. Here are some ways to enrich that soil.

Be a reading family. Read aloud together; read independently. Make reading a centerpiece of your life together. Even young children who are prereaders can enjoy wordless books during their rest time. Read stories, poems, chapter books, magazines, and newspaper comics. Read something that interests you and let your children see you delighting in something you just read.

From the earliest age, sit your child on your lap or beside you and read aloud the wonderful literature, both classic and modern, that is available in local libraries and bookstores. Being read to by a parent brings a sense of peace and security, opens up new worlds and ideas, bridges the gap between oral and written language, and gives the child a desire to read independently. Even teenagers enjoy having Mom or Dad read aloud to them.

Provide lots of reading resources within your child's reach. Make books and magazines accessible and easy to reach: in the family room on a low shelf, in the car on trips, in a big basket beside the bed. Provide a bedside light and a library card. You can build your own family library inexpensively with books purchased at school book fairs, library used book sales, and garage sales. Give a book store gift certificate to your child each birthday and make the outing to pick it out a special time.

Spice your child's life with storytelling. Tell original stories about an imaginary character. Spin tales of your parents or grandparents' courtship and marriage, hard times, and successes. Relate stories from your own personal experience, especially your childhood. Kids love to hear about their parents' first black eye, the time they got in trouble at school, or "when I was your age" stories. Familiar Bible stories, Aesop's fables, true stories from American or world history all are rich resources for storytelling.

When storytelling is a part of family fun and recreation, children tune into language. Research shows telling young children stories actually motivates them to read and write.[6] Their listening and vocabulary improve, their imaginations ignite, and at the same time they develop a great storehouse of information for their own writing while feeling a stronger sense of belonging and roots to their family and cultural heritage.

Children who are consistently told stories by parents and grandparents develop into dynamic little storytellers who love to relate memorable events like their first summer camp experiences or the first tooth they lost. Storytelling doesn't have to be time consuming. There are little spots of time for even the busiest families to tell stories on car trips, while washing dishes, or when taking a walk together.

Encourage pretend play. Pretend play is not just child's play, and it is not a waste of time. It encourages the development of language, vocabulary, and communication skills. Whether it's playing house with a big cardboard box or playing fireman and rescuing all the stuffed animals, dramatic play helps the child begin to realize that

[6] *What Works: Research about Teaching and Learning*, U.S. Department of Education, 1986, p. 25.

one thing stands for another, which is a background for understanding words as symbols (reading) and numbers as symbols (math).

Provide enough time for pretend play and watch your children's imaginations come to life. Many children today are so overscheduled they don't have any blocks of time for just playing with friends. Provide some costumes and props that stimulate pretend play: dress-up clothes from garage sales or Grandma's attic; medical kit and bandages; office props like an old telephone, invoice book, and typewriter; puppets; and all kinds of hats (fireman, cowboy, etc.). You can collect costumes and props in a Make-Believe Box for a terrific Christmas or birthday gift.

Along with pretend-play resources, include pencils and paper to motivate your child (and playmates) to read and write. If they are playing office, they will often write pretend letters. While playing school, they can make a list of their pupils. Playing house calls for the making of a grocery list. Often kids will imitate their parents' vocation in their pretend play.

Provide an Amazing Art Box. A plastic container full of paper, markers, crayons, glue stick, stickers, scraps of fabric, and modeling clay will encourage your child to do lots of drawing and making things. The best readers and writers of today were pencil-and-paper kids who spent much time in their preschool years scribbling and drawing at home.

As your children grow, discover their interests. Does your daughter dream of space and want to be an astronaut? Is she fascinated with horses and other animals? Does your son look up to sports heroes or hope to rescue accident victims like the ER doctors on television? Is your child's top interest dinosaurs, mountain climbing, or computers? There are books for every interest a child could have. A librarian can help search under the topic headings your child is most fascinated with. Whatever makes your child's heart beat faster, get books and magazines on it, for interest is the key to reading success. When they discover books that ignite their center of learning excitement, reading is no longer a chore.

Think "spots of time" for reading. You may be thinking, *When*

THE BUILDING BLOCKS 19

can I find time to read to my child? I'm already swamped with my job, household responsibilities, and carpooling! But there are some ways to make time in overcrowded schedules for reading. One of these is to use waiting times for reading. When you are waiting with your child at the doctor's or dentist's office, carry a new book along and make it a literary event.

When your child is sick, check out a big stack of books from the library, and make a pot of hot chocolate and some warm memories. Besides your own read-aloud times, have other members of the family (siblings, grandparents, baby-sitter) read to the patient. Cuddling up together in bed during convalescence after the flu or chicken pox fills a child's emotional tank more than almost any other activity.

Most children's books are available on cassette and kids can listen to books at nap time, during errands in the car, or on trips. Audio books can be purchased or checked out for free at the public library. Get some blank cassette tapes and make your own: Tape record your voice as you read a new book to your child. Then he can listen to the book over and over again.

Set aside some moments at bedtime to stretch out, relax, and read to or with your child. This little pocket of relaxation can be as enjoyable and refreshing for you as for your child. Once your child is reading on her own, have her read to you, but don't stop reading aloud. Children continue to need to hear phrases and sentences read aloud so they develop an understanding of how language flows. Read more advanced books that your child couldn't read to herself but still finds interesting, because her listening vocabulary is usually way ahead of what she could read herself.

Chapter books are great to read to children, because they look forward to what's going to happen in the next episode, which builds a sense of anticipation for the next night's reading. Discussion of the stories or book is important, as this is how comprehension improves. And be sure to keep magazines and books in sight rather than neatly out of sight because what's out of sight is out of mind. If books are accessible and interesting, you or your child will be more inclined to pick one up and read it instead of flipping the television channels.

All the language experiences your children enjoy at home—listening, conversation, reading, storytelling, questioning, and pretend play—will pay huge dividends and make a powerful impact on the development of their writing skills.

Exercises

1. Enhance listening skills this week by whispering a short message and then asking your child to repeat it or by playing a story on cassette tape in the car and then asking your child to tell you what happened in the story.

2. Put some of your child's favorite books and magazines in a basket next to his favorite place to hang out and relax.

3. What is your child most interested in? Is it whales and dolphins? Then check out a few books on them this week. Is it sports? Trucks and cars? Ballet or karate? Find out what sparks his excitement and get a magazine or book on it.

CHAPTER 3

Providing a Writing Environment

Your home is your child's
most important literate environment.
—Cheri Fuller

Kids are so logical! When we provide the resources and opportunities to do something, they will usually try it: if we provide a swimming pool and lessons, most children will at some point dive in and enjoy swimming. If a horse is in the backyard and someone helps the child to get on and gives a few instructions, eventually he'll probably learn to ride the horse. Likewise, when we provide materials for our children to write with, they tend to discover it's useful and fun. Kids will pick up a lot of the basics of writing if we provide a writing environment. While the chapters that follow will offer many writing activities, here are some basic things you can have in your home that will provide ongoing motivation to write.

Family Bulletin Board

The family bulletin board is more than a list of to-do's. It is a center of communication, a place to keep up with the myriad activities of each person and the group. It's a place to root for each other, to enhance literacy, and use writing on a daily or weekly basis. Besides what you post on the board, encourage each child, youngest to oldest, to contribute to the family bulletin board. It can include:

A quote of the week. Written on a colored index card, a new inspirational quote each week posted on the bulletin board can motivate everybody. The quote could be a thought-provoking idea that leads to a dinner table discussion or a quote that motivates your child to keep trying in a difficult course at school. It could be a humorous quip found on a church or community center billboard.

Where do you find quotes? The *Reader's Digest* "Quotable Quotes" page is a good place to look. Books you're reading, including classic literature, current novels, and nonfiction usually yield words to live by. The newspaper, magazines, and even bumper stickers can be a source of quotes in addition to funny things people say around the house.

Special photos. Candid shots of your kids and pictures from family gatherings and school events give a warm, personal touch to your bulletin board. Your child can write a caption under the photos.

Capitalize on humor. Jokes, cartoon strips, puns, and riddles are excellent additions on your family board. Laughter is the best medicine for all kinds of daily frustrations and disappointments, and frequent doses of it are therapeutic.

Practical stuff. Reminders like "Don't forget to feed the dog!" or "Please empty the dishwasher after school" are best written in a Chore section of the family bulletin board, where they can save lots of nagging and undone work. If you leave such messages for your children, you'll begin to see reminders for you, too, like: "I need $10 for school pictures tomorrow!" or "Could you pick up poster board for my science project today? Thanks!"

Cheer 'em on. Everybody thrives on encouragement, and the family message center is a good place to put it. Notes like "Good luck on your spelling test!" "I know you'll do super in baseball tryouts—We'll be there!" provide support and caring even in the busiest families.

Postcards, photos, and letters from out-of-town family and friends. We always tacked up our latest letter from Thomas, the foreign exchange student from Germany who lived with us one year, or a recent letter from Grandma so everyone got to read them.

Happy day! Whether it's a birthday, national holiday, or one of the lesser-known special days, recognize it and celebrate it on your board.

Family calendar. School open house, piano lessons, sports practices, Christmas programs, trips coming up, and other events need to be written in a central place to keep organized and on track. A calendar can be posted on or beside the family bulletin board for this purpose. "We have saved all our yearly and monthly family calendars," says Vivian, a mother of two. "It's almost like looking back on our history to read what we were doing!" Let each person write in his or her activities on the day of the month they'll take place.

Special people. Post the recent awards like the Citizen of the Month certificate your daughter received at school. Or make up your own awards for Best Helper of the Week or Most Patient to tack up on the bulletin board.

Words in the World around You

Help your child become aware of the print—the written words—all around him in everyday life. This is a constant resource that builds sight vocabulary and word recognition skills. Everywhere we go, there are words—at the baseball game, the discount store, on billboards and businesses as we drive on the streets, in our kitchens, and at the grocery store. Our environment is literally teeming with words and thus opportunities to heighten kids' awareness of language. You can call attention to the printed words at home or wherever you go. Research shows that when parents point out print in the environment, children as young as two can read it.

When you're at the grocery store, read the labels on cereal boxes and other food up and down the aisles. When my children were small, I found the print in my kitchen they were most interested in was on their favorite cereal boxes. Read the labels on canned soups, milk, and cookies. A fun game for kids in the kitchen is to name all the letters of the alphabet they see all around the kitchen. How many A's can you find? How many B's?

Junk mail that arrives almost every day is a good print resource, and children like to write in the blanks, on the envelopes, and copy it. They also enjoy looking through catalogs.

Point out messages, logos, and trade names on people's T-shirts and hats. Take note of license plates and bumper sticker messages and read them aloud when you're driving. Talking about the words you see in the world around you helps your child's awareness of the reading-writing connection and will show him that reading can happen wherever we go.

Then let your child do some labeling. Take some colored index cards and write the name of a few of your child's favorite toys or stuffed animals. Tape the index card labels to the corresponding toys. Your child may want to copy the labels or make her own. Our daughter loved naming her Cabbage Patch dolls and then making name tags for them to wear. Sometimes she made a sign for her room that said, Brothers Keep Out. Girls Only Today!

List It!

One of the most common forms of writing we adults do on a regular basis is making lists. Some of us are compulsive list-makers and feel the need to write everything down on paper or in a planner. Some of us make neater lists than others, but most people catalog tasks or jobs that need to be done at home or on the job, make a grocery list, or a list of items needed to pack for a camping trip.

Kids enjoy list-making because it's quick, useful, and easy. List-making is also great writing practice at home and an aid to their developing organizational skills. You can make your own Things To Do sheets printed creatively and copied at the copy shop, or buy one of the many list pads or sticky note pads available at stores.

Then encourage your child to make her own lists. If, for example, she has a science project coming up that's due in three weeks, suggest she make a list of materials she'll need for the project. "Let's figure out what you'll need to build a model of the eye: styrofoam balls, glue, acrylic paints; what else? Will you need poster board to make your display?" After the supplies are listed, you go out and purchase them.

When birthday time is approaching, suggest your child make a list of people she'll invite to her birthday party. At the birthday party, as gifts are opened, have someone list the gifts and the giver so thank-you notes can be written to each person.

Before school starts, have your child make a list of school supplies he'll need. Usually the teacher of each course gives that information the first day or two of school. Include the items that help organize your child's homework desk, such as file folders (to save tests and important handouts), poster board for projects, stapler, extra paper, and pens.

Each child should develop a system that works for him to keep track of home chores and school assignments. A daily list that he carries to every class and adds to when assignments are made listing textbook pages to read, book report due date, and math problems to complete is essential to excel in school.

When you're going grocery shopping, your child can help by making the list and categorizing what's needed under headings of paper products, dairy products, vegetables and fruits, meat, etc.

Lists for special occasions, like a Christmas list, a list of friends to send Valentines or holiday cards to, a list of places to visit on a family vacation are all fun to write.

List-making helps your child practice writing, keep organized, and feel important. Even young children will feel grown-up by making a to-do list. Here's a list that a mother found in her seven-year-old daughter's room:

CAMMIE'S THINGS
TO DO. RUN. PLAY
ON LANE'S SWING SET
AND DO TRICKS
JUMP THING'S
        —Cammie, age 7

The Writing Center

One of the best things teachers have developed in their class-rooms to encourage composition is writing centers. This puts all the supplies kids need to write in one place so that when an idea hits, they know where to go to write it down. You can make your own home writing center for your child and thus encourage her to write down stories, poems, and great ideas. Provide a place to write—a desk, a lap pad for the bed, a table in the family room, or a big colorful carpet square—and some materials for writing. Some kids like a quiet place to write and others want a desk near music. Ask your child his preferences. Here are some good materials to go in the writing center:

- Sharpened pencils and erasable ballpoint pens
- Markers or crayons for illustrating
- A three-hole binder for storing writing
- Lined 8½" x 11" notebook paper
- Erasers
- A small file box or file folder with writing ideas (you can write some ideas for story writing, poetry writing, or word play on cards for your child to choose from when he can't think of anything to write) and new words
- Some magazine pictures and photos—great for stimulating writing ideas and making collages of words
- Blank books made from folded, stapled blank typing paper with contact-paper-covered cardboard or heavy construction paper covers so that your child can write her own books (Chapter 12 will give easy directions for making these little books and many ideas for bookmaking projects.)
- Stamp pad and stamps of animals, people, holidays, and seasonal stamps (This is optional but fun to decorate letters and stories, or to press the figure of a horse on the page and then write a story about it.)

- A dictionary, thesaurus, and word guide to aid spelling (especially important for fourth grade and up)
- For younger children, an alphabet chart so they can identify the letters they need to write.
- A chalkboard or white chalkless board: Instead of always having to write in little lines on notebook paper, chalkboards are great for writing spelling words, listing jobs to do, drawing, and a score of other things; using their large muscles, kids can experiment with different handwriting or work math problems

When the materials for the writing center are collected, they can be put in an organizer or plastic file box and set on your child's desk or a large project table in the family room. Then your kids won't have to wander around looking for basic supplies. When an idea hits, they will be ready to write.

Computers and Kids

If possible, allow your child access to a computer. A computer is a great tool for young writers. Even five- or six-year-olds can feel comfortable using a computer with a simple word processing program and can learn keyboarding skills from the tutorial games and software. The young writer can save stories, poems, or letters on the hard drive of the computer or a disk, go back to make revisions and check spelling, and then print out as many copies as he wants. With Print Shop or one of the many graphics software programs, your child can make banners that say "Happy Birthday, Dad!" posters, signs, and labels.

Writing on a computer is important for another reason: if a child's fine motor skills are not developed enough to permit fast, neat penmanship, or if a student has memory or learning problems, a word processor is a lifesaving tool for writing reports and doing school work. The word processor is like an extra memory.

Kids who have some memory problems or output problems

(meaning they know the information but have difficulty getting it out on paper, especially on tests or timed essay questions) might find that a computer really improves their ability to write. The editing capabilities of the software frees them from being overly concerned about mistakes so they can focus on what they want to say. If the program has a spell check capacity, that helps students with spelling problems. By the way, those with spelling difficulties aren't alone; even some great writers misspelled words. It was said about Chaucer that he had talent, but he couldn't spell.

Many word processing software programs have these features that aid writing:

- Ability to create outlines
- Adjustable fonts and numbering of pages
- Cut, copy, and paste features for revising and editing
- View a page or report before printing it out
- Built-in graphics (history reports can be formatted to look like the front page of a newspaper or a book report can resemble an old-fashioned diary)
- Software like Correct Grammar by SoftKey and Gram*MA*Tik by WordPerfect checks for grammar mistakes and with Grammar Games published by Davidson a student can learn grammar through games

CD-ROMs (compact disk read-only memory), the plastic computer disks that look like music CDs, store huge amounts of data and are great reference tools. A CD-ROM can hold an entire encyclopedia set with color pictures and sound, dictionaries (there are even talking dictionaries like the American Heritage Talking Dictionary), an atlas of the world, and *National Geographic* magazine. What could take hours in a library to find, a child can locate in a short time with these electronic reference works.

There is also journal-keeping software that includes idea-starters for journal writing like Amazing Writing Machine, published by Broderbund, and Student Writing Center by the Learning Company.

Exercises

1. Collect some materials listed on pages 26 and 27 for your child's own home writing center.

2. Get a bulletin board and enlist your kids' help in decorating it.

3. Give your child some index cards to make labels for teddy bears, furniture, and favorite stuff in her bedroom and to make signs for the door.

CHAPTER 4

Growing up Writing:
Ages, Stages, and Readiness to Write

Kids are not a short-term loan,
but a long-term investment!
—Anonymous

When are children ready to write? Your four-year-old who comes in and shows you a crayon drawing of her puppy with DAG underneath is ready to write. The six-year-old just-beginning reader who tells you stories while you drive around doing errands is ready to write. Children are ready to write in a variety of forms when parents and teachers give them opportunities. Kids are communicating all the time and we can help them most when we understand and respect the skills and abilities they do have, yet avoid discouraging their creativity and interest by correcting their work too early or too harshly.

Although children mature according to their very own inner time clocks, we know that when given the encouragement, models, and materials to write, the normal child will progress through certain developmental stages. Understanding these growth patterns will help you be aware of their readiness and identify your child's stage of writing ability so you can assign or suggest appropriate activities. By no means is the list of characteristics and the suggestions in "What Can They Write?" an exhaustive one, since there is a wide range of behavior in writing that extends over a period of years. However, it will give you a framework or road map with some ideas for things children at each stage might enjoy and how to support their writing.

Preschool and Kindergarten

Basic language patterns form in the preschool years, and children are constantly building vocabulary. From birth through kindergarten, children are in an oral and auditory phase, listening to parents and other adults' word patterns and trying to imitate them. They name objects, begin talking, and recall events, sometimes in great detail. It can take great patience to listen as a preschooler tells you all about what happened at the park.

Preschoolers begin to have a sense about sequence in events and can dictate stories orally. By age three, most children can distinguish between pictures and written symbols. They scribble messages and notes with great enthusiasm in a left to right pattern like adults do. They expect parents to be able to quickly decipher their scribbles, and sometimes get upset when they can't.

Drawing and scribbling are important prewriting activities through which kids express their ideas. As they draw, fingerpaint, and color, they also develop coordination and fine motor skills. Some preschoolers can write the first letter in a word as they are explaining below a picture what it's all about, and when they do, the letter represents the whole word. As they progress through kindergarten, they may write letters for the first and last sounds of a word, and later begin to hear and add letters for the vowel sounds inside words. Thus some young children at this stage are beginning to use invented spelling. Since they do not know the conventional spelling for all words, they make up their own spelling. Here's a note my daughter Alison wrote when she was five years old:

I Love you Mommy
When I wuz ur Baby (beside a picture of a heart and a baby sucking its thumb)
Now I am a Bllrena grll (with a picture of a ballerina)

A note to her brother said:

Alison Fuller	Chris Fuller
Sad	BeHape
(underneath a picture of a girl crying	and a very happy girl)

Don't be alarmed. In only two years she had advanced to more conventional spelling with her story about a rabbit:

I had a rabbit. It is big. It is cute. I like it a lot! My rabbit had a cut on his ear. I put some ice on it. My bunny plays with me. I gave it some food. He like that a lot! I had to go to bed. My bunny got to sleep by me. I liked that. So did he! I love my rabbit.

This also shows Alison's use of imagination, because we never did have a rabbit as a family pet. Her command of the English language continued to develop as she read and wrote in school and at home.

Here are some more important considerations about children in kindergarten: They tend to dictate stories of approximately five to ten sentences orally; they are aware of left-to-right direction of letters and symbols on the page and aware of spacing (in sentences and words). They also like to retell stories from literature or children's books and dictate stories for pictures they've drawn.

WHAT CAN THEY WRITE?

When your toddler or preschooler begins to scribble or write, show her how to hold the crayon or marker. Respond positively to early attempts at writing or drawing, saying things like, "I like what I see you writing," or "Would you like to draw or write some more?"

Preschoolers can, with a little help from Mom or Dad, make their own books and tell wonderful stories. As you take dictation, your child's imaginative stories can be turned into books with covers of cardboard or construction paper and pages sewn or stapled (see chapter 12). Young children love to make "All About Me" books in which they choose five or ten photos from babyhood to the present, put them in chronological order with a little help, glue or tape them into a book, and then tell you what is happening in each picture so you can write it underneath (or they can write it themselves in invented spelling).

Diana Purser, formerly a high school English teacher in Zwibrupcken High School in Germany, said that the best thing she ever did to encourage her daughter's writing was to make a book of the story April had told. "When April was about four years old we made our first 'book' together. It was three pieces of typing paper, trimmed and stapled. April dictated a story to me about a princess in a castle. She drew and colored some pictures to go with the story. It was a small book, but a great beginning. April loved it and we saved it in her baby book." April enjoyed the project so much that she wrote many other books, but that first one remains her favorite.

When you help your child make a book—when you put her words on paper—and then read the book back to your child, something powerful happens in her literacy development: She begins to under-stand the reading-writing connection, the relationship between the spoken word and the written word. The rereading of personal writing is a vital aid in learning to read. Your child watches the words as they are read to her. She knows they are her words and wants to remem-ber them and this increases her interest in telling stories and learning to read. Since kids like repetition, you may hear the same story line over and over again, but along the way she is gaining confidence.

Plastic letters of the alphabet which have magnets on them to stick to the refrigerator or a magnetic board are good tools for experi-menting with word-making. You can provide a cookie sheet with sand for the child to draw and make letters in. And with little pads of paper and invoice books near their toys, preschoolers will naturally incorporate writing into their pretend play.

Rhythm and rhyme come naturally to most children, so they enjoy hearing and creating simple poems. You'll find some of the poetry projects in chapter 15 work well for young children if adapted to their abilities, such as dictating to a parent who records their words, or composing a poem together. Word play—riddles, jokes, and tongue twisters—is not only fun for young children, but makes them more aware of the sound and rhythm of language.

Another important step of preschool writing development involves learning to write their name. Many kids are eager to do this, but rather than pushing him to copy his name over and over or forcing the issue, wait until your child wants to write his name.

Although preschoolers may be developing early language skills and may not be able to write, it is never too early to build a strong foundation for a love of writing.

WRITING ACTIVITIES FOR PRESCHOOLERS AND KINDERGARTENERS

- Draw and scribble
- Dictate stories of all kinds
- Play alphabet games by shaping letters from play dough or clay, make letters in sand, shaving cream, or dry jello
- Make an "All About Me" book and create other books dictated to parent (See chapter 12 for directions)

First through Third Grade

First graders, just like kindergarten children, tend to write in the same way they play with building blocks, clay, or anything else—just for fun. In other words, they write for the sake of the activity, rather than for the final product. They rehearse their ideas and stories by drawing and talking about them. They may invent their spelling or write with a combination of conventional and invented spelling. When given the freedom and opportunity to express themselves, they can often produce delightful poems, stories, and even plays. When a second or third grader does dictate a story orally, it has approximately ten to twenty sentences.

In grades two and three, students begin to write letters and invitations, simple reports, directions (how to get to a friend's house or how to make a peanut butter sandwich), and descriptions.

At the early stages of writing and reading, many children's writing is slow and takes much effort as they are trying to manage the pencil. Written stories may be shorter than stories your child dictates to you. You can strike a nice balance between your child's growing independence and desire to write for herself and your taking dictation. Let your child's creativity continue blooming (she will likely use more vivid, descriptive words and elaborate on the story more when dictating) by alternating: one time she writes the story down and another day you take dictation while she tells the story.

Spelling may appear to be poor (by adult standards) when children write their own stories down because they are sounding out words and they may have little recognition of punctuation or capitalization. This is not the time to correct your child's story and insist she rewrite everything over to get it right. More important, celebrate her writing by displaying it, or publishing it by copying it and sending it to grandparents. Children are quite sensitive in their desire to not be wrong, and if parents continually correct invented spelling, they tend to stop writing.

Children in the lower elementary grades may show some letter reversal or writing backward; don't worry—it doesn't mean the child is dyslexic. A mistake in spelling made by your six-year-old won't be forever ingrained in her mind if you allow it to go uncorrected. Spelling is a developmental skill. As they begin to read more, gradually they will begin to incorporate conventional spelling into their writing. By fourth or fifth grade, if they have had many reading and writing experiences, children will have learned how to spell most of the words they need to express their ideas in writing, so their editing skills will begin to improve.

As John Holt said, "The best way to spell better is to read a lot and write a lot. This will fill your eye with the *look* of words, and your fingers with the *feel* of them." If children do lots of reading and writing for pleasure, he says, spelling skills will improve because they will get better, clearer word images in their minds.[1] For children who continue to have spelling problems as they get older, Holt suggests taking the misspelled words from their own writing and making spelling cards. On one side of the index card, print the word. On the

---

[1] John Holt, *Learning All the Time*, NY: Addison-Wesley Publishing Company, Inc., 1989, p. 36.

back, draw a picture of the word or tape a magazine picture of it, and include a sentence in which the word appears. The child can review these spelling cards and check his writing with them.

By the second and third grades, children usually begin to develop some sense of audience, especially if they have opportunities to share their writing at home and school (with handmade books or anthologies or sending in their writing to the kids' page of the newspaper). Some children tend to move toward more conventional spelling and even attempt editing by grade three. They want to get things right because somebody's reading it.

Third graders' stories become a little more complicated with a plot, sequence, and dialogue. They like to retell familiar stories. They become aware of titles and try to create one for each story they write. They also are interested in writing for a variety of practical reasons like listing friends for a party or gifts they hope to get on Christmas or passing a note to a best friend at school asking her to sleep over.

WHAT CAN THEY WRITE?

Besides the many ideas throughout this book that can be adapted to early grades, children love creating treasure hunts for friends or siblings. The child writes clues on slips of paper for the hunter such as: "Your next clue is in the living room by something *red*." "Look under a place where we eat snacks." "Beside the birdhouse is your treat!"

Second and third graders also love making original greeting cards and invitations. Give your child brightly colored construction paper, stickers, cut-out pictures from magazines and old greeting cards, a gluestick, glitter, etc. Let him create birthday cards, Valentines, or holiday cards and write his own greeting or poem inside. He can also make his own birthday party invitations.

A spiral notebook with a collection of words to use in their writing is helpful for second and third graders. Besides new vocabulary words, they can have a page for feeling words, seeing, tasting, hearing, smelling words, verbs, some vivid synonyms to use, adjectives that would enliven their writing, etc.

Introduce letter writing to first and second graders. If early writers are encouraged to write thank-you notes after birthdays and Christmas or to send postcards to friends and family while on vacation, it becomes second nature. The chapter on letter writing gives many reasons to write letters that appeal to not only first and second graders but children of all ages.

Interest in writing about fantasy, out-of-this world things, and make-believe people is at a height at this age. Enjoy this magical age and the writing that emerges.

Activities and Writing Projects for First Graders
- Write letters and simple words using different media: thick markers, paint, glitter
- Write first and last name, capital and lowercase letters of alphabet
- Dictate or write stories to explain pictures
- Dictate or write a friendly letter or make a rebus message—a message using pictures to resemble the intended words or syllables
- Write and illustrate books
- Retell a familiar folktale
- Write lists such as: My Best Friends, My Favorite Animals, What I Want to Do This Weekend

Activities and Writing Projects for Second and Third Graders
- Write stories of own experiences or fantasy
- Write friendly letters and address envelopes
- Write thank-you notes and invitations
- Make lists of Things to Do, Friends, Favorite Foods
- Write simple directions such as How to Get to My Friend's House
- Write a short report on a topic of interest
- Write poems, especially color poems and sensory poems (see chapter 15)

- Write a paragraph describing a person or place
- Play treasure hunt game and write clues
- Write a book report
- Write and illustrate original books (see chapter 12)
- Keep an illustrated journal that includes sketches, magazine pictures, and comic strip cut-outs

Fourth through Sixth Grade

Vocabulary continues to build so that by fifth grade, children can usually spell most of the words used in their writing. They revise for better meaning and mechanics. They write stories several pages long with conflict, characterization, and often lots of dialogue. Whatever kids read tends to turn up in their writing. If they read a lot of poetry, they write lines that rhyme and experiment with poetry. If they read a Star Trek adventure, they try to write science fiction. This is a good age for the child to learn to take notes, to do research by using reference materials, the dictionary, and a thesaurus, and to write factual stories.

Fourth to sixth graders can write reports, charts, diagrams, and descriptions. They particularly enjoy writing personal experience stories and fantasy stories, new versions of old folktales, and letters.

At this age children write more uniform letters with better punctuation and capitalization. They are more aware of the standard of what is correct and thus have a higher awareness of errors. They write faster and begin to proofread their own work. At the same time, they get discouraged easily and often groan when told they have to write a rough or first draft and then a final copy, especially if the assigned writing is a longer piece.

In most states, there are writing assessments at fourth or fifth grades, and at this level they contain both narrative and expository writing. At sixth grade, persuasive writing is added. Middle grade kids write book reports and are interested in getting their ideas and opinions on paper. They also enjoy writing a play and then acting it out, collaborating as coauthors, writing with a group, or writing alone.

WHAT CAN THEY WRITE?

Encourage journal keeping. Besides being excellent writing practice, a journal is a terrific outlet for a young person's feelings and ideas. Provide a blank book and suggest your child fill it with what happens at school and home, events on trips, hopes and dreams, or any of the many ideas for journal keeping listed in chapter 10.

Expert territory. Whatever your child is most interested in and can become an "expert" on can lead to writing opportunities for the fourth through sixth grader. If your daughter is interested in space, she can write NASA for information on how to become an astronaut, visit a space center, and then write about it, or participate on ASTROFORUM through the Internet, communicating with others who share her interest. If your son is excited about sports and sports cards, he can send his cards and request autographs from professional players, subscribe to a magazine like *Sports Illustrated for Kids*, or write a sports column for his school newspaper.

This favorite interest or area your child is an "authority" in can produce an informative how-to essay on something he knows how to do, such as: "How to Make the Best Chocolate Sauce in the World" or "How to Collect Rocks and Minerals" or "How to Build a Rocket."

Try a learning log. This kind of writing particularly appeals to the science/math-oriented child. In addition, fourth to sixth graders are often interested in the facts, so keeping an ongoing record of what he is learning as it takes place encourages both his thinking and writing skills. In his own style and language, your child can take notes on a hiking adventure and record the autumn things he sees and collects. An older child can record the methods and results of his rocket experiment or the dam he constructed. Another student may keep a log of the weather over a certain period of time. The learning log is a good place for writing observations: what people looked like underwater while swimming, what the moon looked like at several stages during the month. He can also describe problems, note discoveries, clarify concepts, and record ideas for future projects.

Show your child how to use writing as a way to organize and

retrieve important ideas and information. He can practice by jotting down a summary of a chapter he's read in a book or by trying to write down the minister's three main points made in a sermon on Sunday morning.

One of the best ways to support young writers of any age is to break down the writing task into manageable goals. Just like you eat an apple one bite at a time, if it's a long piece of writing (like a three- to five-page report, which may seem long to a fifth grader), do it one paragraph or page at a time. Set aside plenty of time for the project. Have the child spend the first few days reading and taking notes. One day can be devoted to putting the information in some kind of order using an outline. Then a few days can be focused on writing. By scheduling each task needed to complete the project, the child is less likely to be overwhelmed and can avoid the pressure of having to do it all at the last minute.

Activities and Writing Projects for Fourth through Sixth Graders

- Interview a grandparent and write a family history story
- Write book reports (see creative book reporting ideas in chapter 9)
- Write fantasy, mystery, or science fiction stories
- Experiment with writing different kinds of poetry: limericks, tongue twisters, haiku, sensory poems, and color poems
- Keep a journal
- Write letters for free stuff, travel information, etc.
- Use E-mail to get information for reports and hobbies
- Use E-mail to keep in touch with a pen pal
- Write a how-to paper: "How to Make a Pizza" or "How to Breed Tropical Fish"
- Imaginative diary writing (for example, create five diary entries writing as someone from another time in history—a passenger on the *Mayflower*, a child during the Civil War, a crew member of the first spaceship to land on the moon.)
- Keep a learning log in science, math, or other subjects, to record observations and experiences from field trips, experiments, etc.

- Write personal experience stories
- Research a topic and write a report with several sources, including CD-ROM information, books, interviews, etc.

Junior High and High School

The typical junior high writer can organize and compose an essay, a story, or a report. Seventh graders and up are more independent in their writing and their letter forms, and punctuation and capitalization becomes more consistent. Writing flows more easily, the student's vocabulary is wider, and he is more descriptive. Self-evaluating and correcting develops as they learn to edit and revise the first draft into a polished final copy. Writers at this stage aren't just interested in the ideas and expression; they begin to care more about the final product. If they have been shown the writing process and had practice with it, they are able to move through the steps of prewriting, drafting, revising, and editing, and they particularly enjoy getting to publish or share their writing with a larger audience.

WHAT CAN THEY WRITE?

If your teen has written something interesting, creative, or humorous at home or school, a terrific way to encourage her writing is to offer a wider audience. Seeing her writing in print is not only exciting, it can lead to interest in writing as a profession.

There are over a hundred magazines that publish young writers' work, and dozens of writing contests each year. In chapter 16 I will share some specific guidelines on preparing writing for submission to a magazine or contest.

Teenagers can also improve their writing skills by engaging in on-line activities through the Internet. Jonathan, a fifteen-year-old, has many on-line friendships and keeps up with his endless list of friends around the country by E-mail. "On-line has helped me to do research for articles and school reports," says Jonathan. In fact, he has traveled to Washington, D.C., to do an interview with the administrator of the FAA and some experts in the field of aviation. He got the interviews by meeting someone in Washington over the Internet who helped him set up the meetings. Writing a newsletter in the area of his special interest or being on the staff of the school or local newspaper can also be a great activity for the teenage writer.

The high school writer should have some practice in composing well-organized expository papers, descriptive essays, and narrative pieces. He should now know how to write a research paper using library resources. (Although middle school students start doing research writing on a small scale, the high school writer is more independent and advanced in his ability to use reference tools.) In the process, he is expected to take notes on note cards, outline the material, document footnote references used, and make a bibliography. By the end of high school, writing skills should be solid and competent.

Doing informative and persuasive writing is where most students fall down in national or local writing assessments, so it's a good idea to include this in your writing program. Informative writing includes a process paper, in which the writer explains how to do a task, and an opinion essay. The opinion essay is friendly persuasion in which students have to state their opinion on a controversial issue and then back it up using facts, figures, concrete evidence, and relevant incidents. Adolescents often have strong opinions about a number of issues, and this gives them an opportunity to express those constructively.

Activities and Writing Projects for Junior High and High School Students

- Write descriptive essays.
- Use E-mail and Internet resources to pursue interests and get information for reports.
- Write an informational how-to paper ("How to Build a Bench," or "How to Be the Best Baby-sitter in Town").
- Write a newspaper or magazine ad.
- Help write a newsletter or a class/school newspaper.
- Using library resources, write a research paper. Take notes on

index cards, compose an outline, and write a composition of five to ten pages including a bibliography and footnotes. (Shorter report of five pages in seventh to ninth grade. Full ten-page research paper by senior level.)

- Write an opinion essay, in which the student states her opinion on a controversial issue and backs it up with evidence, statistics, and specific detail.
- Write business letters: cover letter for job application, letter asking for information, etc.
- Write in a variety of forms and tones (such as serious or humorous), and for different reasons and audiences (such as letters, diaries, poems, stories, essays, directions).

Encouraging Words

At every stage and age, when children write, they need our encouragement and affirmation rather than criticism. Encouragement can come in the way we respond to the ideas our children express in writing. If we are sensitive, attentive readers and focus on content, asking questions like, "Can you tell me more about this story?" "What's going to happen next?" "How did you think of this interesting character?" then our kids will continue writing, risking, and enjoying the learning process. Take a positive approach and always find something good to say about what your child has written. It might be a descriptive word he used, an interesting twist at the end of the story, neat handwriting, or word pictures. Handling their writing with respect fosters a good self-image and a sense of trust. Then next time he writes something, he'll be likely to share it with you.

Exercises

1. Choose a writing activity that corresponds to your child's age and developmental level and then do it this week.

2. Have your child make a list of subjects, sports, hobbies, activities, or things he or she is an expert on, i.e., really knows about and

is somewhat of an authority. Have him keep this list in his writing folder or journal because it will generate many topics for writing. Here is nine-year-old Jennifer's list:

- Bicycling
- Writing limericks
- My grandparents
- Taking care of little sister Jessica
- Eating pizza
- Planning fun sleepovers
- Playing soccer

3. If your child is in a school, ask the teacher what writing activities and projects are going on in the classroom and see how you could reinforce these at home.

CHAPTER 5

How Writers Write:
Understanding the Writing Process

> *Writing is similar to stroking a tennis ball,*
> *baking bread, building a sturdy shelf,*
> *sewing a dress, planting a garden. It is a process*
> *of making, and it is fun to make something well,*
> *to handcraft a piece of prose that will carry*
> *meaning and feeling to another person.*
> —Donald Murray

One of the top ways to support your child's writing is to help him understand the natural steps professional writers go through to produce a story, article, or chapter of a book. Whether the writer is a newspaper journalist, television writer, poet, or magazine writer, he or she tends to go through a sequence of activities. These stages are called the writing process, and although there are different working styles and ways of writing, for most writers it consists of:

- Prewriting
- Drafting (writing the first and successive drafts)
- Revising
- Editing and proofreading
- Sharing or publishing

If we give students an assignment to write something and say, "Here's the topic. Write a page on it. Turn it in tomorrow," it's a sure recipe for writer's block because we've left out some important elements of the writing process. But if we allow them to enter into the process of writing, the results are amazingly positive.

Allow me to share the process I go through when writing a piece for a magazine. First, after getting the assignment, I talk to the editor and get her input about what she wants in the article. Then I spend time thinking about my topic and what direction I want to go with it. This thinking time may be in my office, at the bookstore over a cup of coffee, or outdoors as I walk my dog. Next, I may begin to brainstorm on a piece of paper, listing all the people I want to interview for the article or places I can search for information. As I pull out resources from my own library and files and read them, I take lots of notes. I talk to other people who know something about my subject or I may dialogue with Melaine (a fellow writer), my husband, or a friend about it.

Then I begin the interviewing process, calling the people I've listed, asking them questions, and typing the interview as they talk. I may also surf around on the Internet to pull up some recent research or statistics on my topic. Whew! Sometimes it seems like a lot of work—and I haven't even started writing the article yet. But research is necessary and it can be fun—it's like putting together pieces of a puzzle. After several days of this prewriting stuff—of reading, thinking, interviewing, talking, jotting down notes, and writing down whatever comes to my mind about the topic—some ideas will begin to emerge about how I'm going to organize the article. If I've done a thorough job of prewriting, the article will generally flow when I sit down at my computer. Then, as I begin to write the article and find I'm missing information or need to interview some more people, I go back and do some more prewriting.

I go to my keyboard with all my resources and notes on hand and begin to quickly draft the article, not stopping to do major revisions or make every paragraph perfect. If possible, I try to write the first draft in one sitting, especially if it's not a long chapter or article. When the first draft is written, I print out the story and then switch gears and work on another project or do a couple of chores—anything to take a break from the project. An hour or even better, a day later, I go back to the story with a more objective view.

I read the article with pen in hand, crossing out, adding words, rearranging phrases. I write in the margin, above lines, inserting a paragraph or sentence to make my meaning clearer. I may delete whole sentences or paragraphs and within a short time, the piece may be unrecognizable or at best, extremely messy, with all the revision marks. I go back to the keyboard and input the changes and print a new copy out. That night I may ask my husband or someone else to read the in-progress article and ask him for honest feedback. Then I incorporate his suggestions, perhaps changing the lead to better hook my readers into the story. Editing, proofreading, and polishing the manuscript come later, after I get the ideas and content to flow smoothly and clearly.

Prewriting

When we don't allow enough time or ways for kids to engage in enough prewriting strategies to get their ideas flowing and yet expect a polished piece of writing, the result is frustration and a strong sense that "I'm not a good writer. I can't write."

In contrast, I find that when we do invest time and show children ways to prewrite—giving them a variety of strategies like clustering, storytelling, drawing, mapping, interviewing, taking notes, researching, talking with friends, and others described below—then the whole rest of the writing process goes smoother and they feel more confident whether the project is a poem, story, or research report. Prewriting is the stage where the topic is selected and ideas are generated, when the writer decides who he's writing the piece for and what he's going to say.

How to Help During the Prewriting Stage

A free exchange of conversation is helpful in the beginning. For example, if your child has to write about a personal experience, you could review what's been happening lately and have him make a list: his aunt's wedding, being tutored in reading, helping Dad clean up the garage, and having a sprained ankle. He decides the sprained ankle he sustained while bouncing on the trampoline sounds like the most interesting possibility for a story. Since talking is a good way to rehearse his story before writing, have him tell you what happened first, how he fell, how the ankle hurt. If he's having a hard time explaining, have him draw a picture of what happened first, second, and third and then tell you the story. Drawing and making maps and sketches are good ways to prewrite and rehearse ideas, as I demonstrate in detail in chapter 11 on writing scar stories.

If the topic assigned is a report on science, connect the topic to your child: what he's an "expert" on or knows something about. Everyone likes to write about a topic they can relate to. If it's a general topic, help him narrow it down and find a connection. If a report needs to be written on insects, for instance, go to the library and have him look at some books on various types of insects. Encourage him to pick an insect that really interests him. As he reads and looks at photographs and diagrams, he can begin to collect ideas and details to jot down.

Direct, hands-on experience before writing is terrific for many kids. If your child has a paper to write on seashells, you could visit an aquatic museum or tide pool. If you're lucky enough to live near a beach, he could look at and hold a variety of seashells and experience their environment with the five senses. Drawing some pictures of seashells or looking up information in an encyclopedia about shells and then talking about it is also helpful.

Clustering is another wonderful way to generate ideas. Clustering (also called webbing) is a right-brain method that taps the mind for ideas and words, associations and connections. Suggest he write the core idea in a circle in the middle of a page. Then, with lines going out like the spokes of a wheel, he quickly writes down around the subject-circle the ideas, feelings, words, phrases, and anything else he can think of related to the topic. See figure 1 for a cluster on the word *scared*.

At this point, don't stop the flow of ideas by saying, "No, that's not a good idea," or "There's no use writing that word down; it's too hard to develop." Instead, help him look for connections between the ideas, examples, and details after the original cluster is made. After a

figure 1

few minutes of clustering, he could try freewriting on one of the words on the cluster. Clustering can lead to creative thinking and problem solving—and even develop the ingredients of a poem, story, or report.

Another prewriting strategy involves asking the newspaper reporter's questions of *who, what, where, why, when,* and *how* about a topic. Put the key word "The Battle of the Bulge, World War II" in the center of the paper. Then draw lines out from the circle to a *who* circle (which armies were involved in the battle, key generals, etc.), a *when* circle (the date the battle took place), *why* or *what* caused the conflict, etc. Use the five *W*'s and *H* to collect information and details while reading and researching.

When brainstorming, who should write the ideas down—parent or child, teacher or student? The ideal is for the young writer to have the pen and jot down ideas as you both talk. If you're one of those people who thinks best with a pen in your hand, you could say, "I'm writing this down so I'll remember the ideas and because I think better this way," but encourage your child to do his own clustering, drawing, or note taking.

WHAT TO AVOID IN THE PREWRITING STAGE

Avoid taking over, selecting the topic, and writing the paper for your child. When parents are overfocused on the final product (the report or story and the grade he's going to make on it), they tend to skip the process, jump in, and do too much, thus derailing their child's efforts and motivation.

What we want to teach our kids is how to engage in the *process* of writing, because this is where so much learning takes place. In this part of the process called *prewriting*, we want them to know how to generate ideas, or what to do before writing the first draft, and most of all, to figure out what really works for them.

Anything you can do in the way of clarifying ideas, asking questions—"Are you saying this?" "It sounds like you're interested in writing about this."—or helping him talk about what he wants to say or what he knows is more useful than saying, "Here's what you need to write on." As you help your child discover the prewriting methods that work best for him to generate ideas—such as drawing, mapping, reading and researching, or storytelling—it will pay off the next time writing is assigned.

Writing the First Draft

Drafting is the go-for-it stage of the writing process. After your child has drawn pictures of the beginning, middle, and end of his sprained ankle experience and told you the story, now it's time to get all the ideas down on paper. You can tell your child to just get the story down. Pour the words out. Don't worry about every word being spelled correctly or right punctuation yet. Just do it! Pretend you've just called your best friend and said, "Here's what happened to me." Let your personality and excitement come through just like it would if you were telling the experience to your close friend.

How can parents and teachers help at the drafting stage? Give lots of encouragement. Comments like, "Your ideas are good. This is an interesting topic. You can always change or correct it later, so just put your story into words" are supportive.

Let's say your child is working on a report on Abraham Lincoln. He's finished reading several biographical sources and the encyclopedia; he's clustered and brainstormed on what is most important in the character and career of Lincoln; he's talked with you and clarified his ideas. Now encourage him to write down everything he wants to say about Lincoln. Too much is better than not enough. He can always pull out the best after he has gotten his ideas out or he can write another version if he doesn't like what he has written.

WHAT TO AVOID IN THE DRAFTING STAGE

Although you want to help your child and take an active role in encouraging her to write, don't become too involved and take the pen out of your child's hand and write the first draft of the story or report for her. As parents, we want our kids to succeed, and consequently I've read a lot of reports and stories coauthored by parent and child (or written by the parent when the student procrastinated until ten P.M. the night before the assignment was due and Mom didn't want her to get a zero on the assignment). But a high grade on the assignment isn't worth the result: totally squashing her confidence and initiative as a writer ("I guess Mom thinks I can't write this so she's writing it for me.") or increasing her dependence on you.

When your child begins to write the first draft, get out of the picture; don't correct or dictate what she needs to write. Be encouraging and assure her that her ideas are good and worth writing down. The goal is to get all the writer knows or wants to say out and then to go back and revise.

REVISING

Revising means refining or making improvements in the *content* (not mechanics, spelling, and specific grammatical errors, yet; that comes later during the editing stage) of the first draft of the story, poem, or report. It's when we try to make what we have written *clear* for the reader. "Remember that though you start by knowing what you mean," said C. S. Lewis in his advice to a young writer, "the reader doesn't, and a single ill-chosen word may lead him to a total misunderstanding. In a story it is terribly easy just to forget that you have not told the reader something that he wants to know—the whole picture is so clear in your own mind that you forget that it isn't the same in his." [1]

One of the best ways a writer can begin is to let the first draft sit and get cold, either by working on some other homework, taking a break, or even waiting a day to revise.

Then have the writer read the first draft aloud to a partner—either you, or a sibling, friend, or even to himself on cassette tape. Our ears catch things our eyes miss. Once a writer hears the sentences aloud, he can better spot the problems. I always share with young writers one of the first wise sayings I learned at a writing conference: *All good writing is rewriting*. I show them the various drafts of an article I wrote for *Family Circle* magazine, my changes, and the editor's changes so they can see that real writers *rewrite*. Perhaps you could show your child a first draft of a letter you wrote for your job, or correspondence to a congressman or the principal and how you marked it up and revised it.

Questions are helpful in the revising stage, both from the writer and the one listening to the story:

- What is the part you understand best?
- What is the part that isn't clear? At any point of the story did you get mixed up?
- Are you saying . . . Did you mean . . . ?

The writer can decide through this dialogue what changes to make in the first draft. First he wants to make sure the main points or main parts of the story are in logical order and make sense. The writer should also consider:

- Would a person who doesn't know anything about this subject understand what you're saying?
- Is there something you want to say differently or make clearer?
- Does the paper read smoothly?

[1] C. S. Lewis, *The Essential C. S. Lewis*, ed. Lyle W. Dorsett, NY: Collier Books, 1988, p. 522.

- Is there a paragraph you've repeated that needs to be deleted or something that needs to be added?
- Do you have a clear beginning, middle, and end to your story or report?
- Have you *shown* the reader how you felt, what the scene looked like and sounded like or did you *tell*: "When I sprained my ankle I felt bad." What sensory details could you add to help the reader see, hear, touch, and feel what you did?
- What else in the story needs work?

Using some of the above questions—not all of them at once because that could be overwhelming—make a checklist to act as a general guide for revising. Brainstorm on the best title and see if the lead sentence of the story makes the reader want to read on.

WHAT SHOULD WE AVOID IN THE REVISING STAGE?

Since the author is supposed to be making the decisions on what changes to make based on the feedback he receives from a partner or "editor," avoid too much criticism at this stage. If errors are pointed out too soon, too harshly, or too often, children won't keep trying to write. Keep your comments encouraging and supportive like, "What an interesting topic. I've already learned some new things by reading this," or "I can see you've given this topic a lot of thought," or "You've done a good job getting a lot of ideas down." The worst thing we can say is, "Your ideas are wrong, and I know how to fix them." Just as damaging to the aspiring writer would be if he's written some strange and fantastic outer space adventure and we say, "Why don't you write something other than fantasy?"

Rewriting is about learning to look for the strong and weak parts of a story and deciding what to add, delete, and rearrange so the writing will be more clear. It's about risking and trying something different. But revising is not about making the writing perfect. In the next stage, editing, you can work on correctness.

A computer is a great help to the revision process because it makes it much easier to add, delete, or move words and paragraphs around. Help your child learn to type on a keyboard. When he gains skill in doing editing, revising, and spell checking on the computer, a lot of the drudgery of revision disappears and he'll enjoy making changes in his writing much more.

Editing and Proofreading

Our goal in editing is to help young writers move toward more independence so that they are eventually equipped and confident to be responsible writers: to proofread their own writing, to confer with another person, and to correct as many spelling and mechanical errors as possible, thus producing a readable piece of writing. Yes, correctness is important, but arriving at it is a process, and it should not be done at the cost of smashing a child's interest and love of writing. Here are some ways to work toward that goal:

Have the author read the story aloud again to you or encourage him to work together with an editing partner. While reading his sentences aloud, he can catch where the natural pauses are and thus where punctuation is needed. You can say, "Let's see what sentences are too long, without a pause for the reader."

If this is a school assignment and you don't know the teacher's expectations or what the paper is going to be graded on, ask. Is she taking points off for spelling errors, misused capitalization, and sentence fragments? Is she giving two grades, one on content, the other on mechanics? When you find out what the emphasis is on, make out a checklist of five to ten things to proofread for on the paper, considering your child's age and language skills.

If you are a home school parent, decide what you want to pay particular attention to in spelling, punctuation, and sentence structure and then make the checklist accordingly. (See "Guidelines for Assessing Your Children's Writing" in the appendix to help with your checklist.) Concentrating on a few grammatical errors at a time usually works better than trying to tackle all the mistakes in one writing assignment. Remember that all writing doesn't need to be turned in and graded. Every story or poem doesn't need to go through the whole editing and revising, polishing, and publishing/sharing process. Instead, do regular daily writing (journal writing, stories, poems, etc.) and then pick one or two pieces of writing every week to follow through the whole process.

Here's an example of a proofreading checklist you might make for a third grader before she writes the final copy:

- ☐ Does each complete sentence have a period or an end punctuation mark?
- ☐ Did I check for sentences run together with a comma?
- ☐ Did I start each new sentence with a capital letter?
- ☐ Did I use the words *you, your*, and *you're* correctly?
- ☐ Did I check for spelling errors?
- ☐ Did I use the words *there, they're*, and *their* correctly?

Here is a second grader's editing checklist:
- ☐ Does my story make sense?
- ☐ Have I read my story to at least two people?
- ☐ Have I used capital letters for names of people and places?
- ☐ Have I used punctuation at the end of sentences?
- ☐ Have I circled the words that I think I need help on?

On each paper or writing assignment, you can adjust the checklist to reflect what the child needs to be learning: using colorful modifiers and vivid verbs, varying the way you begin and construct sentences, using transitional expressions to make the story flow smoothly, combining choppy sentences to make longer ones, etc. You may find you need to provide some skill instruction along the way.

For example, if your child frequently runs sentences together with a comma or no punctuation at all, you could do a mini-lesson on comma splices. Take several sentences from a children's book and remove the periods at the end of sentences. Write the sentences down run together and ask your child to read them aloud deciding where punctuation needs to go.

This is where grammar handbooks and workbooks come in handy.

If there is a pattern of a certain error, like comma splices, find exercises on it and have your child complete them. Then, on the next checklist, make the first item: Did I check for sentences run together with a comma or without a period?

Have your child start his own list of frequently misspelled words and check over the list to make sure these are correctly spelled on stories and compositions.

WHAT SHOULD WE AVOID IN THE EDITING AND PROOFREADING STAGE?

Avoid overwhelming the writer with too many grammatical and mechanical expectations or being too harsh in your correction. If you are teaching your child at home, find out what are realistic grammar and spelling expectations for your child's age and development. We can't expect kids to know things they haven't been taught or to apply grammar rules they don't understand. The more they read and hear good literature and correct English, the more children's own command of language improves. Pick a few mechanical or grammatical mistakes to deal with in each paper rather than ten or fifteen.

See the "Grammar Guide" in the appendix for help on teaching your child basic grammar skills. Also, get a good grammar handbook for home use or that is a part of your child's writing center. This handbook should contain information, standards, and examples on parts of speech, punctuation, capitalization, usage, commonly misused words and phrases, subject-verb agreement, etc. Among the many grammar guides available on the market are:

The Essentials of Grammar by Hayden Mead, Ph.D., and Jay
    Stevenson, Ph.D. (NY: Berkley Publishing, 1996)
Essential English Grammar by Philip Gucker (NY: Dover, 1996)
Guide to Grammar & Punctuation: A Writer's Handbook by Leonard
    J. Rosen (NY: Barnes & Noble Books, 1985)

Encourage your child to make frequent use of his pencil eraser and the edit and spell check features on the computer to rewrite, change, and enjoy improving his story. Careful proofreading becomes more important to kids when they have an actual audience they are going to share their writing with. Below in the publishing stage we'll look at many ways they can share their writing and thus see the need for correctness. The more kids know that someone is going to be reading their work, the more they care about polishing it.

Instead of overreacting to errors and mistakes, which causes anxiety, remind them that we all make mistakes. Don't expect a perfect paper, especially from young writers.

Focus on content first, on what the writer is saying and how he's saying it. Make available an English handbook (which you can find at bookstores or in a library) to look up grammatical errors and methods of correcting them, and a spelling or word guide to check potentially misspelled words. If your child is writing for school, find out how much involvement the teacher expects and recommends on homework and writing assignments.

And in the editing process, it's just as important not to take the pen out of your child's hand and fix or correct the composition. When we take the pen and do all the changing, we assume ownership for the writing and the child's motivation takes a nosedive. Reading aloud with pencil in hand, he can mark the errors while you confer, making notes of any ideas on how to change them, then rewrite or type the paper in the final form.

Some questions you can use to help point out grammar, word choice, and punctuation or spelling errors as you confer with your child are:

- Do you think a different word might work better here?
- Have you started each new sentence with a capital and used capitals for all proper names?
- Do you think this is one sentence or two sentences run together? Where might a punctuation mark go?
- Are you sure this word is spelled correctly? Why don't we look it up in the dictionary or word guide?

When my children shared their school or home writing with me, I often had to tie my invisible English teacher's red pen hand behind my back; otherwise I would be tempted to correct all their mistakes for them instead of letting them do the editing. I purposed to focus and comment on what they did right in the paper—the fresh word used, the interesting information they'd gathered, or the metaphor that struck me at the end of the poem. Then we conferenced together using some of the above editing strategies, working on one major error at a time. I tried to remember that writing is personal, it's a process, and most of all, the paper or assignment belonged to them.

Publishing: Sharing Your Child's Writing

When I use the word *publishing*, I actually mean *sharing*, and it's what makes the whole writing process seem worthwhile: giving someone else the pleasure of enjoying what the writer has composed, revised, and edited. Stories and poems are meant to be heard and enjoyed by readers, just as songs are composed to be sung, not stuffed in a drawer or closet. So the more ways we can help kids share their writing, the more motivated they tend to be in getting it right. In chapter 16, we'll explore many of the markets and contests for publishing children's writing in magazines across the country, plus how writing should be submitted for publication.

But let's look at some other ways to share writing that are right in our own homes and backyards. Reading a story aloud at dinnertime, making it into a little book, including it in the family newsletter, posting it on the family bulletin board, or copying it and mailing it to grandparents are all good ways to share writing. Making puppets and acting out the story for the neighborhood can be fun. One child I know reads his stories to the elderly people at the nursing home he and his mother visit weekly. Another E-mails his current writing to fellow young writers for their feedback and participates in on-line forums where adult authors can answer his writing questions.

Entering an essay in a local newspaper's contest or including a recent piece of writing in a letter to a friend gives other people a chance to read your ideas. When we give our children the opportunity to share their writing, the writing comes to life. They begin to see the reason to put effort into revision and editing. And sometimes a future writing project is inspired.

Exercises

1. List some of the prewriting strategies in this chapter that you think would best help your child generate ideas and warm up before writing.

2. Have your child pick one of his current pieces of writing that he has the most interest in or holds the most promise to work through the rest of the writing process: drafting, revising, editing, and publishing. Choosing one essay or story a week out of the many things a child may be writing in a journal or for daily assignments is more realistic than trying to revise them all.

3. Together with your child make up two checklists: one for revising that might include clarity, structure, word choice, and content; and an editing checklist to cover punctuation, grammar, and spelling. These lists will be a guide for his rewriting and an assessment tool for you.

4. Pursue one of the ways listed above for your child to publish or share her writing, such as mailing a story to grandparents or reading aloud at the dinner table.

CHAPTER 6

Writing Letters for Fun, Friends, and Profit

A pleasant letter I hold to be the
pleasantest thing that this world has to give.
—Anthony Trollope

When I was six years old, I discovered my great uncle lived in Juneau, Alaska. Since Alaska was not yet a state and was a long way from Dallas, Texas, it sounded like a fascinating place to find out about. Eskimos and igloos were things I'd only seen in photographs in a geography book. So when Uncle T. P. wrote me a letter and enclosed several photos of the frozen city of Juneau in winter and him ice-fishing with his Eskimo friends, I was hooked on writing letters and remain an avid letter-writer to this day.

After receiving that first letter, I prompty answered it, sharing the family news and asking Uncle T. P. questions. Before long, the mailbox held another letter from Uncle T. P. to me. Thus began our lively dialogue across the miles, which provided several essential elements to my development as a young writer: a reason for frequent writing practice, an audience to write for (with the added benefit that on my uncle's yearly trips to Texas, he took me out for a fancy steak dinner instead of any of my five siblings), and feedback on what I was writing.

Writing letters became part of my lifestyle, as regular and normal as any of my other activities. Soon after, I initiated a correspondence with my maternal grandmother who lived in Houston, and when school friends moved away, I knew how to not lose touch—I wrote letters.

What happened to the art of writing letters? When telephones became a fixture in every home in America, the practice began to drop off. Whereas in past decades, people's whole lives had once been chronicled through their letters, many families today have no written record of their or their parents' lives. But it's not too late to resurrect the art of writing letters and let our children enjoy the benefits. And the benefits are numerous:

- Fluency in writing increases. Developing writing skill is much like developing facility in a foreign language. The more a student can speak with others in French, for instance, the more fluent she will become in the language. Similarly, it takes a lot of writing practice to become fluent in written language and regular writing of letters is a perfect opportunity.

- Writing letters is terrific practice for all kinds of other writing and can lead to skill in both fiction and nonfiction. Alex Haley, award-winning author of *Roots* and other novels and screenplays, discovered his talent for writing while aboard Coast Guard ships in his years of duty. He began writing love letters for other sailors to send home to their girlfriends, and his career was launched.

- Well-written letters show colleges, prospective employers, and scholarship programs that you're a good communicator.

- As we write letters to a trusted friend or family member, we find our own voice and discover what we think as we write. Thus, writing is a discovery process.

- It makes a child's day to receive mail. Supportive relationships through exchanging letters can mean much to a young person. Letters can be sent by "snail mail" (U.S. Postal Service), by fax, or by E-mail. And they can be saved and enjoyed over and over.

Ideas to Stimulate Writing Letters

Unfortunately, although writing letters has terrific benefits for your child and is the writing we need most in real life, it is the least stressed in school. So much of the writing students labor over in the classroom—filling in blanks in a workbook or answering questions on a book report form—gets marked and then stuffed in their desk, locker, or the garbage can. But letters—written, stamped, and mailed—get feedback and response, the magical element that motivates people to write more. How do you get your child to write letters? Here are some ways:

• Provide your child with an address and telephone number book with entries for friends, family members, and classmates.

• Ask a family member or friend who lives in another state if she will be willing to write to your child on a regular basis. It could be a grandparent, aunt, cousin, or family friend. What a great way to build a relationship! I correspond with two teenage nieces in Texas and enjoy hearing about their world and their concerns.

Encourage the person who is writing your child from time to time to stick in little comic strips, quotes, jokes, riddles, or anything else of interest.

• Provide letter-writing materials that are easy to get to. It could be something as simple as a basket or plastic tote on the bedroom desk that includes: a pad of writing paper, pens and pencils, envelopes, and stamps. Children love having their own personalized stationery with their name at the top (a good holiday or birthday gift, which can be created quite inexpensively at the local copy shop). Add some colorful stickers and markers to the letter-writing tote. With decorative stamps and stamp pads, your child can even design her own creative stationery.

• If you have a computer and your child has keyboarding skills, letters can be typed, graphics added, and the whole thing printed out in no time. Or if he's fascinated by a high-tech approach, try communicating by E-mail (see the next chapter).

What Kind of Personal Letters Can Your Child Write?

THANK-YOU LETTERS

Grandma will faint when she gets a note from your child thanking her for the birthday gift. A thank-you note is proper etiquette and has special meaning for the person receiving it. Yet, showing appreciation is almost a lost art. Thanking people for gifts can become a wonderful habit if each year you give your child a box of thank-you notes in his Christmas stocking, and then a few days later, have everyone sit down for an hour and write notes of appreciation for the kind gifts they received.

Let your kids see you writing and sending thank-you notes, little impromptu ones that say, "Thank you for the extra help you gave Jenny in math this week! It really made a difference and we appreciate your teaching" that your child hand-carries to her teacher. In addition, slip a note on your child's pillow that says, "Thanks for helping me with the groceries and dishes today when we had company coming. I couldn't have made it without you!" Your example might lead to your child's expressing thanks to others.

FAN LETTERS

Kids love to write to celebrities or sports heroes. Ask your child who his favorite television or movie star is, and then provide the address. He can send off the sports hero's baseball card to be signed and returned for added fun. Your child might like to write her favorite author, especially if she's enjoying a series of the author's books. These can be addressed to the publisher of the book who then forwards the letter to the author. One young reader I know writes a letter to the author when he has just read and really enjoyed a book. In return, he's received a letter back from an astronomer, astronaut, and some of his favorite children's writers.

FRIENDSHIP LETTER

There's nothing more fun than getting a letter from a friend who lives in another place. Two friends can read the same book, like

Madeline L'Engle's *A Wrinkle in Time*, and exchange ideas about the plot in their letters. They can write about news, ideas, television programs, camp and school experiences, and myriad other things.

INVITATIONS

Invitations are good letters for beginners because they are brief and announce a birthday party or special event. Encourage your child to include the five *W*'s on the invitation: *Who* is having the party? *Where* will the party be held? *When* will the party start and end? *What* kind of party (include any special costume that's to be worn)? And perhaps *why*, or the reason or occasion for the gathering. The party information can be written in a letter form or creatively grouped in a balloon shape. A pretty or bright color of paper can contain the final draft, and don't forget the R.S.V.P. with your phone number so guests can respond if they are coming.

ENCOURAGEMENT, APOLOGIES, OR GET WELL LETTERS

Letters to someone who is in the hospital or who has had a recent loss, illness, or difficult time are always welcome. Sometimes we need to apologize for something and a letter is a good way to say "I'm sorry . . ." Everybody needs a little encouragement from time to time. Sharing what you appreciate about them or just saying "I love you" can make someone's day.

I remember a letter my daughter Alison wrote me at age nine just to send a little comfort:

To Mom,

I am so very sorry that you got a rejection! But you are the very best writer in the whole world!! I'll try to help you around the house and even try my hardes to not gripe or complain!

I love you so very much!

Love ya,
Alispie

LETTERS ASKING FOR INFORMATION OR FREE STUFF

One of the most motivating reasons for children to write letters is to get free materials for a hobby or interest. There are hundreds of free and inexpensive things kids can send for by mail, from Neon Frog Paper to a free Texas Rangers or New York Yankees fan pack, science experiments, and model skeletons. Hobby materials, history and geography stuff, space stuff from NASA—lots are available by just sending a postcard or letter requesting free stuff.

Here are some addresses your child can write to which will yield some interesting packages arriving at your house before long:

Stickers 'N' Stuff
Department KC
P. O. Box 430
Louisville, CO 80027
Will send twelve metallic-chrome stickers of animals

H & B Promotions
Department 90 SRC
P. O. Box 10
Jeffersonville, IN 47130
For $1.00 they will send a Louisville Slugger bat pen

Federal Reserve Bank of New York
Public Information Department
33 Liberty Street, 13th Floor
New York, NY 10045
For a comic book on money, the economy, and finances

Newton's Apple Science Try-Its
c/o Twin Cities Public Television
172 East Fourth Street
Saint Paul, MN 55101
For six free science experiments

There are a number of books that list hundreds of addresses and things kids can send off for like: *Free Stuff for Kids* (published by The Free Stuff Editors, Deephaven, Minnesota), *Free Things for Campers and Other Lovers of the Outdoors* (G. P. Putnam's Sons), or *Freebies for Kids* (Wanderer Books). Also, check your local library's *Books in Print* for current books that list addresses for free stuff. Almost any child can get fired up about writing letters when something fun and free is the reward, so this is a great reason for writing.

Make sure when writing for free materials that your child:

• Writes neatly, requests free stuff politely, and thanks the person.
• Encloses a SASE (self-addressed stamped number ten or large envelope) for the reply or the stuff to be sent back. Without a SASE, some materials or answers will never arrive back to your child.

PEN PAL LETTERS

Having a pen pal in another country can be a terrific reason for correspondence. Here are some addresses for pen pal services that connect children in America and abroad:

Student Letter Exchange
630 Third Ave.
New York, NY 10017
(212) 557-3312

Skipping Stones: A Multicultural Children's Magazine
P.O. Box 3939
Eugene, OR 97403
Besides featuring art and writing by kids all over the world, *Skipping Stones* will connect children who want to have an international pen pal.

When your child writes for a pen pal, have her tell what country she'd like or what language she is studying at school, her age, school, and address. A small fee of a dollar or two may be required.

LETTER TO THE EDITOR

If your child subscribes to a magazine, encourage him to write an occasional letter to the editor expressing an opinion on an article or feature. He may even receive the pleasant surprise of having his letter published in the magazine. If your child doesn't receive a monthly magazine, find one in the area of his biggest interest and give a subscription as a gift or read it each month at the library. The regular reading of the magazine is a boost to language skills, and many children's magazines have a page for readers' contributions, letters, poems, jokes, etc.

Letter Writing for Younger Children

Even prereaders can start writing letters, if you are willing to act as the scribe. A young child may want to start by dictating a letter as you write it down, and then illustrate the letter or decorate it with a sticker. Then when she receives a reply letter addressed to *her*, what excitement! As you read the letter to your child, she learns a little more about the reading-writing connection.

Encourage your child to write a letter to the Tooth Fairy, Santa Claus, or the Easter Bunny by dictating it to you or writing the letter in invented spelling. These are wonderful letters to save in a scrapbook.

Children of all ages can create personal greeting cards if you provide some bright construction paper, markers, crayons, or colored pencils, and perhaps a stamp pad and stickers. Homemade greeting cards are fun to make and receive, and with a little help and encouragement, any child can make one. Older kids can use their cards as a way to share poems, artwork, and creative thoughts and ideas.

Postcards from the Kids

Picture postcards with a short message are a great way for children to stay in touch with their friends and relatives. Since there's only a small amount of room to write, a postcard isn't intimidating and even the reluctant writer will tackle it. When on a family trip, let your child pick out a postcard at each place of interest, write a short message, and mail it to a friend or family member back home. Even a prereader can pick out a postcard and dictate a message for you to write.

Children can also use their imagination to make their own postcards to say hello to grandparents or tell what they did on vacation. You can buy some blank postcards at the post office and then let your child decorate them with stickers or an original illustration and write a little message while riding along. Busy hands are happy hands in the back of the car!

You can also purchase postcards with adhesive on the front side to attach color photos to. On the back is a place for a message, plus the name and address of the recipient. Grandparents love these.

Writing the Personal or Friendly Letter

Encourage your child to write letters that are conversational, interesting (not the "How are you; I'm fine," over-and-out type of letter), and neat enough to be easily read. Perhaps you could compose the first few letters together, always being respectful and supportive of your child's ideas. When you write a letter to a friend, read it aloud to your child and ask, "What do you think of this? Anything I should add or change?"

Help your child picture in his mind's eye the person he's writing to and think about the letter as a little visit. It helps some of us if we can picture that person across the table as we chat over lemonade. Encourage him to ask questions and show interest in the person he's writing (What have you been up to? What do you think about this new movie?), to include something about what he's doing at school, at home, and in sports, and to write the letter in a conversational, not a stilted style, just as he would talk to the friend.

Although friendly or personal letters to friends or family members are usually written in a casual, conversational style, there is a format that should be followed.

- The *heading* includes your address and the date, written in the upper right-hand corner.
- The *greeting* or salutation usually starts with the word *Dear* and the person's name you are writing.
- In the *body* of the letter, you express clearly what you want to say. The body is usually divided into short paragraphs for easy reading.
- The *closing* appears two lines below the body of your letter and is followed by your *signature*.

Name
Address
City, State Zip
Date

Dear Grandma,
   (or Hi, Carrie! or other friendly greeting or "Salutation")

Body of letter follows:

_____
_____
_____
_____

_____
_____.

Love,
(or Your friend or another warm closing)

Chris

- The envelope for the personal letter contains: the return address (name on first line, street address on second line, city, state, and zip code on the third line) in the upper left-hand corner of the envelope.

Centered on the envelope is the name, address, city, state and zip of the person who will receive the letter.

Alison Daniels
5910 Oak Cliff Road
Oklahoma City, OK 73192

Jenny Jarvis
12466 Sligo Road
Yarmouth, Maine 04096

A good way to help your child proofread the letter before sending it is to have her read it aloud to see if what she meant is what the letter actually says, and to see if a period ends each sentence and a capital letter begins each new sentence. Although you wouldn't want to insist that your child do several rewrites on a letter to a friend until the letter is perfect, you can encourage neatness and correctness with the motivation being that you want the person reading the letter to be able to easily read and enjoy the message.

Business Letters

When your child needs to write a letter to order materials or ask for information, write a letter to the editor of a magazine, or a letter to a prospective summer employer, it's just like a visit to that businessperson's office. Since the typical office worker or manager tends to be busy, the letter needs to be clear and to the point. Encourage her to use a form similar to the friendly letter with these differences:

Add an *inside address,* which is written right under the date line. The inside address contains:

Line 1: The person's name you are writing
Line 2: The company name
Line 3: The street address, P.O. box, and suite number if one exists
Line 4 City, state, and zip code

• In most cases, black or blue ink on white paper is used for business letters, rather than hot pink ink on colored stationery. Neat printing or typing is preferred.

• In a business letter, both the salutation (greeting) and the closing is a little more formal and the salutation is followed by a colon:

Dear Sir: or Dear Ms. Spengler: (instead of Hi, there!)
Yours truly, or Sincerely,

• Always thank the person you are writing to show your appreciation for the time they took reading the letter and handling your business like: "Thank you for your help" (or information, or consideration).

Keeping in Touch

Whether you're away from your child because of your work or because she's at school, little everyday notes and letters are a great way to not only show you're thinking about her, but to motivate her own writing. Consider these easy ideas:

• Write a lunch box love note that says something like "Have a terrific day at school. Let's get ice cream afterward! Love, Mom." Slip the note into her lunch bag or box and watch your child's smile after school. Even before he can read all the words, begin to write notes to your child combining easy words he can recognize with pictures. In doing so, you create a rebus (combination of pictures or symbols and words) message perfect for the prereader to figure out. His curiosity about language will be stimulated and he'll find a way (or someone older) to help decode the message. Then as your child grows, he will likely begin to surprise you with little notes of his own, like the one I received one morning years ago from my son, Chris, when he was three:

MOM—I LOVE miy mom and miy mom love me.
LOVE Chris

He's six feet three inches and in college now, and I still treasure that note among my keepsakes.

• Write a note in code. Make up your own number or symbol code and write a message (with a guide to the letters represented) and put it under your child's pillow when you go out for the evening. Kids love to break the code and figure out the message.

• Write Camp notes. When your child goes to camp, write a different short note for each day of the week (or every few days if camp time is more extended). Put each note in an envelope, number the envelopes, and hide them in various places in your child's suitcase or trunk. They can be short reminders or encouragers like: "Make a new friend today! And enjoy every minute . . ." "We're thinking of you." "Don't forget your sunblock when you're swimming."

• Use a white chalkless board in your child's room to write notes, suggestions, or directions for using her time while you're working or busy with a project.

• When you're out of town, select a postcard at each destination, write the highlight of the place you visited that day, and send it to your child. If you have a fax machine at home and you're traveling, you can also fax a quick message from the hotel to your child or send E-mails via your laptop computer.

• Notes under the door: Writing notes to your child is a powerful way to boost your communication and strengthen emotional connections. When the teenage years arrive, you'll be glad if you've already established a custom of writing notes to one another. Notes like "Don't forget to take out the garbage" or "You forgot my allowance this week!" can replace nagging and defuse irritations. Notes can help you keep track of your teen's hectic schedule: "I went to Kathy's, then soccer and play practice, so I won't be home for dinner tonight."

Note-writing can get you through some rough spots in your relationship. When my daughter Alison would occasionally hole up in her room and get frustrated with her family, friends, and/or the whole world, she could write out her feelings in a note or letter to me, which helped me understand what she was going through and how to help. Adolescents can sometimes accept our displays of love and affection better in a letter than in our arm around them at the mall (especially during those "Please, Mom, I don't want them to see you hugging me!" years).

Notes are great for apologies, "I'm sorry I lost my cool last night. Forgive the spill-over of my stress on you!" They are ideal for expressing encouragement when our kids experience disappointment over failing to make the team or making a low grade after hours of study.

Sally Rubottom, one home school mother I know, writes a note to each of her school-age children at the end of the home school year giving them a loving evaluation of the year, especially praising them for the progress she observed.

Writing the reasons that your child thinks she needs an allowance increase, why she should get a VCR of her own for Christmas, or requesting permission to go out of town for the weekend can prevent arguments and can be good practice in persuasive writing. And all these activities show your child that writing letters and notes is an important way to keep connected with someone you love and that writing is extremely useful in everyday life. In the next chapter we'll look at the benefits of using high-tech letter-writing or E-mail.

Exercises

1. Make a family mailbox for children and parents to exchange personal notes and letters.

2. Have your child send off for something free this week.

3. Suggest your child write a letter to someone who made a difference in his life and who may not know about how he or she helped or encouraged him. It could be a teacher, coach, grandparent, or anyone who has been a special friend.

CHAPTER 7

Write Away! Using E-mail to Boost Your Child's Writing Skills

One thing that amazes me is how fast electronic signals can go through a phone line!
—*Andrew T, age twelve*

When Richard and Penny Hook spent a year and a half in Beijing, China, they created a written journal of their experiences called *China Letters* with 190 E-mail messages written and transmitted to their parents, brothers, and friends. From getting off the airplane with their three children to the family hike on the Great Wall of China, the children's string recitals and school events—everything was shared with family and saved, later to be printed out and bound in a special memory book. While in Beijing, they also received over 225 letters from Richard's family.

"We knew what was going on in each other's lives almost on a daily basis although we were thousands of miles apart," says Richard. Before they would have had a once-a-week phone call with his parents, brothers, and their families in Oregon, but with E-mail they were in much closer touch.

Their children, Leslie and John, also wrote their grandparents and friends in Oregon, Oklahoma, and Texas, and received many E-mail letters of their own in response. It was the perfect way for the whole family to share the adventures they experienced in China. "All our children can use E-mail," says Richard. "And since the messages are composed off-line, the cost stays cheap."

Write Away! E-mail and Letter Writing

What the Hooks have tapped into is one of the safest and best educational uses of the computer: E-mail, or electronic mail, where you can send and receive messages through your home computer, using a modem and phone line. It's like sending and getting regular mail in your mailbox, but much faster.

More than thirty-five million American homes and thousands of schools are plugged into technology through computers, but most people are missing out on the uses that can benefit children's learning. "The most important thing about computers in education is to use it in a fashion that students have control over instead of the computer controlling the child," says Dr. Glen Bull, University of Virginia professor. With electronic flash cards, for example, the computer controls the child, leading her to the next screen and the next concept. But with word processing, the child has control. And once kids have facility with word processing, they can start to use the computer for a tool to expand their academic capabilities—exploring the encyclopedia on CD ROM or E-mailing the Library of Congress or writing regularly to an international pen pal, for instance.

Although much has been said about the dangers of kids in cyberspace, a major way to safeguard your family is for the parent to take the time to learn about how computers, modems, and on-line services work so you can monitor your child's use and help your child use the computer as a homework helper instead of just a video game machine.

E-mail: The Benefits

There are terrific benefits when children learn to use E-mail for communication and information gathering. Students can E-mail the Library of Congress for material on the American Revolution for a school report. They can transmit a letter to the editor of a children's magazine they subscribe to or even submit a poem or story and see it in print in next month's issue. They can send thank-you letters to Grandma for the birthday gift, get information on rocketry or science questions, and develop a pen-pal friendship with a child or relative in another country, all via E-mail.

When Oregon sixth grader Andrew Tunnell's older brother spent last summer studying at a German university, they found E-mail an easy way to keep in touch. "Every other day we'd E-mail each other. My brother would tell me what site he visited that day and some history about it." Not only did Andrew's typing and writing skills improve dramatically over the summer, but he learned a lot of interesting information about another country. One homeschool teen I know has *30* E-mail penpals all over the U.S. and world, which supplies her with consistent, weekly writing practice.

Writing for an Audience

E-mail has particular value because everyone communicates better if writing for a real audience instead of just the teacher's red pen. When I sit down to write to my daughter, I imagine her reading the letter, laughing when I relate something funny our cat Princess did or smiling when I share some good news. It becomes a conversation between the two of us. When kids write through E-mail, it's almost as if they can picture their pen pal on the computer screen, and it is even more immediate than a letter. They gain excitement for and skill in written communication with every letter they write. The sense of audience increases when the message composed off-line is E-mailed to four cousins or friends in different places at once, and then the sender gets an E-mail back within that day. The pride kids feel as they successfully convey ideas into words and get feedback spurs them on to correcting, rewriting, and struggling for better words. Writing letters helps children develop vital critical thinking skills.

Word processing on a computer has dramatically impacted the writing process and paved the way for children and adults to write with less frustration. Even children with a learning disability or with fine motor skill problems, which make handwriting a struggle, can find expression more possible and enjoyable on a computer.

E-mail: A Boost for Busy Parents

E-mail has plenty of pluses for parents, also. You can keep in daily touch with your child's teachers. You can send an E-mail letter to far-away family or friends, keep in touch with college kids, create a family newsletter and send it with a click to twelve relatives at the same time. And in doing so, you're resurrecting the lost art of writing letters and creating a written history of your family.

When you have to be out of town on business you can still keep in close touch with your children. Barbara, a U.S. Customs official, E-mails her children every day whenever she has an international trip and they share what's happened that day at school. An Oklahoma dad I know sent and received regular E-mails from his three children during his recent business trips to Moscow. When Dave, a New Hampshire dad, had to be in Florida for a trip, his son sent him his school report to read—using the fax option on his modem, and Dave received it moments later in the hotel office and was able to respond to him almost instantly with some positive encouragement.

The computer can become a writing center, an information center, and a correspondence center for the whole family. More than anything else, the example you set is vital. When children see parents and siblings using E-mail for real-life reasons, they are motivated to try their own messages. Since fluency and skill in writing are directly related to practice, E-mail activities like the ones below provide lots of reasons to write at home. Your involvement as a parent is essential both to your child's safety on-line and his learning how to tap into the best educational use of the technology.

Close relationships and activities between you and your child are vital to prevent your child from depending too much on the computer for fun or chat. When they do log on, here's how you can help your children get the most out of computer time.

PROVIDE GUIDELINES AND GROUND RULES

Tom Lough of Simsbury, Connecticut, allowed his son Kyser to E-mail a friend he met at summer camp, but he set some house rules: ask for permission each time you log on; don't ever leave Basic Services; anything dealing with adult language is off limits; and don't ever give out their password. He and his son moved from joint sessions where he helped Kyser log on, to Tom reading a book nearby and checking on Kyser. He showed him how to get information from the library for reports and continues to stay involved with his son's on-line activities.

In addition, monitor *to whom* and *how often* your child sends E-mail messages. You don't want him missing out on valuable playing, talking, homework, or reading time by being on the computer too much. Although it can be a terrific learning tool, a computer can never substitute for the need kids have for quality time spent with parents. Set a limit on the time you will allow your child to be on-line and the number of E-mails your child can send in a week, and then post it on the computer. If you do subscribe to an online service, be sure to check whether the service offers pornography of any kind. If they do, complain and consider canceling your subscription.

Last, teach your kids not to give out personal information or say anything in an E-mail that you want to keep private. Since E-mail travels over phone lines and through many computers, the messages could be read by strangers. *Caution your child never to give out her real name, home address, or telephone number.*

TEACH YOUR CHILDREN NETIQUETTE OR ON-LINE MANNERS

Courtesy is just as important when writing E-mail letters as it is in person. Discuss with your children these netiquette suggestions so they will practice politeness in print:

1. Answer your E-mail promptly and politely, and in most cases, briefly.
2. Address E-mail letters properly, using the person's correct title such as "Dear Librarian" or "Dear Editor" and use an appro-

priate closing such as "Sincerely, Kathy" or "Your friend, Brian."

3. Don't write in ALL CAPITAL LETTERS. It's just like SHOUTING!

4. Encourage your kids to use complete sentences and to end each sentence with a dot (keyboard term for a period).

ENCOURAGE E-MAIL ACTIVITIES THAT BUILD LITERACY AND LEARNING SKILLS

There's lots of fun stuff to do on-line that gives children great opportunities to read, write, and learn. Check the current year's Internet Yellow Pages, World Wide Web directory, or a similar resource at the library for current electronic addresses.

Here are some on-line activities that are educational and fun:

• *Tap into Libraries*. Meghan, a seventh grader, did all her research for her report on Thomas Jefferson by E-mail. She was even able to download some historical documents from the Library of Congress to add to her resources. Local and university libraries can also be contacted for research and information through E-mail.

The Library of Congress welcomes students' use of its searching and services when the information sought is unique to the Library of Congress. For example, the Library of Congress contains historical collections and rare works such as the original Declaration of Independence, speeches by Thomas Jefferson and George Washington, and early and current records of the Congress of the United States on legislation. If the request needs specialized resources in the Library's collections, they forward it to the appropriate person and respond quickly. If your child's request can be answered by local public, college, or university libraries, they encourage you to use those resources first. To reach the Library of Congress, Library Stack, E-mail to: http://lcweb.loc.gov/.

• *Ask a question about the rain forest, an almost-extinct species of gorilla, or other science and geography questions*. E-mail National Geographic, WORLD, NASA, or another science organization. Check the magazine or materials from the organization for a current E-mail address.

• After reading and discussing an important national or state issue together, encourage your child to E-mail your congressman with her opinion. First read up on the issue in your local and regional newspapers, talk about the pros and cons of the issue, and then, after some thoughts are formulated, send them. Call your local office of state congressmen and senators for their E-mail addresses.

• *Develop a friendship with an E-mail pen pal.* Having an international pen pal has always been a great way to learn about another country. But often with the two- to six-week delay in receiving letters, the penpal relationship bogs down and most kids lose interest. E-mail solves the time problem. Once your child is connected with a pen pal in another country, he can learn about another culture and the differences in school, family, and lifestyle. In a matter of minutes the message reaches its destination to the pen pal's home or school computer, even if it's 10,000 miles away, and your child gets a quick response instead of waiting for weeks.

Ask for an E-mail pal by E-mailing your child's name and age to one of the children's discussion groups such as KIDFORUM (an international discussion group for ten- to fifteen-year-olds). Send a message to the E-mail address listserv@vml.nodak.edu with the text "subscribe KIDFORUM Your Real Name."

• *Create an electronic family newsletter.* Let your child be the news reporter, gather family news, and even interview Granddad and other relatives. Encourage him to include some family history trivia, Grandma's favorite recipe, funny family sayings, reports of new babies born, trips taken, and cousins' soccer triumphs. Then he can write it all up (composing the newsletter off-line) and E-mail it to the whole family with a click of the Send key. This first publishing venture is exciting for children because they can receive feedback from caring adults and get the bug for journalism. There's more about how to write family newsletters in the next chapter.

• *High-Tech Storytelling:* Your child can enjoy high-tech storytelling with a friend via computer and modem. The first author starts a story about a deep-sea voyage or an adventure in the rain forest. She writes a paragraph or a page of the story and E-mails it to her friend. Author number two picks up the story and uses her imagination to create the next part. The coauthors take turns until the story is finished, then print it out and illustrate their book.

• *Connect with the global village.* Schools and home schools can connect with classrooms all over the world. "Kids having contact with kids in other places in the world is very powerful," says Dr. Judi Harris, University of Texas professor and specialist on students' learning on the Internet. One exciting project involved a classroom of children who communicated through E-mail with a school in a Nicaraguan village. Through communicating via the Internet, the American students discovered that the village had no running water and that some children had to walk seven kilometers twice a day to fetch the family's water by hand, so they couldn't attend school. The U.S. students decided to raise money to purchase a water pump for the village. They raised $200 U.S. dollars to send to a foundation that installed the water pump.

Within a few weeks they received an E-mail letter from a fourteen-year-old girl, thanking them for enabling her to go to school because she didn't have to spend her day hauling water.

• *On-line Mentoring.* Through a program called Electronic Emissary, volunteer experts are paired with children or teacher/classrooms who want to learn from them, and they communicate through E-mail. One match was a fourth grade girl who was very interested in Arthurian legends. She had learned what she could from a school unit and the local library, so her dad put an announcement on the expert database Electronic Emissary for someone who could teach her more about Arthurian legends. A professor responded, delighted to share his specialty with this young student. A lively interaction, teaching, discussing, and questioning ensued between the young student and the history professor.

NASA astrophysicists are mentoring science classes through E-mail messages, in which the scientist sends activities, answers questions, and sends CD-ROMs to the class he is mentoring. Professional children's writers are responding to young authors' manuscripts and sharing writing ideas. The sky's the limit for the learning available on-line! (To connect with Electronic Emissary, visit their Web site at: http://www.tapr.org/emissary. After reading the information available on the Web page, you can E-mail them with specific questions. This is one of the best educational opportunities on the Internet, and it's absolutely free!)

USE E-MAIL TO STAY INVOLVED WITH YOUR CHILD'S EDUCATION

Most schools have computers and many have modems and are on-line, allowing students, teachers, and parents to stay in close touch. Ask your child's teacher if she has an on-line address, then ask for and send E-mails to keep updated about what the class is studying. You can inquire about how your child is doing and how you can work with her on a problem area. The teacher can respond at her convenience.

Many universities now supply students with computers and free Internet access, so you can also keep up with what's going on with your college kids. While Kathy's son was at Naval Academy, they were in daily touch via E-mail, which helped provide him with needed support from home and eased her transition of having him 2,000 miles away.

By getting on the information highway and using E-mail yourself, you'll quickly get over your fear of the on-line world, set a good example for your children, and at the same time help your child get the most out of the computer and become an expert communicator.

Welcome to the Information Highway

On-line services such as America Online, CompuServe, Prodigy, Genie, and others tend to be easier to navigate on than going out on your own with an independent Internet provider, and they have many features students can use to boost their learning, research, and home-work efforts like:

- Organizations such as NASA, National Geographic Society, Sierra Club, and the Smithsonian Institution have information for many school subjects.
- Encyclopedias, magazines, and newspapers from all over the world are available on-line.
- Forums and discussion groups for children interested in politics, star gazing, baseball cards, the movies, or almost any hobby are available.
- Educational publishers have excerpts of books, reviews of books, anthologies of stories, and other materials and resources for research.
- You can hunt for college scholarships, find information about colleges and universities, and even do job and internship searches on-line.

Check with your on-line service for the educational opportunities available to children and teenagers. Then log on and learn.

Exercises

1. If your home computer has E-mail, log on with your child. Either write someone an E-mail message and send it, or E-mail one of the sites listed in this chapter.

2. Check on the E-mail capabilities of the computers at your child's school and at the local public library. Find out what projects the students are doing on the computer and suggest one of the on-line learning activities discussed here.

3. Next time your child has a report to write, suggest he do some of the research via computer and E-mail.

CHAPTER 8

Across the Miles: Writing Family Newsletters and Neighborhood Newspapers

Our families are a circle of strength and love.
With each birth and every union the circle grows.
Every joy shared adds more love. Every crisis
faced together makes the circle stronger.
—Anonymous

Barrett and Ian, Texas nine-year-olds, decided to write and distribute door-to-door a weekly neighborhood newspaper they called *Highland Park Herald*. For fifteen cents a copy, the folks in their community could read about upcoming garage sales, who had a new baby or new puppies, who's on vacation and where they went, soccer victories, and other stuff people might want to know. One issue contained a story about a family of raccoons that took morning swims in a neighbor's pool. Another included a piece on the Fourth of July block party and parade.

A moneymaking project for Barrett and Ian, they used the profits to buy baseball cards and special army men they wanted. They gathered stories by going door-to-door in a four-block area and asking people if they had any news they wanted to share. Ian's mom keyed in the information in her computer. In addition to sixteen stories per issue and letters to the editor, their newspaper included ads for community businesses at a cost of $5 for one month. The local copy shop gave them free printing for free advertising. What a deal!

Keeping Friends Connected

When Lauryl was in the seventh grade, she had twenty pen pals she wanted to keep in touch with, but found it hard to write twenty letters on a regular basis. So one day she sat down at her grandparents' computer and composed a one-page letter to all twenty friends. At the end of the letter she asked if each would take a department—stories, recipes, editorial, current world issues, interviews with people, etc.—and submit something under that topic each month. Many of them contributed stories, and Laurel's three-page newsletter, *Sisters*, was launched.

Her mother designed a logo, and Lauryl got great feedback from her readers about how much they enjoyed the features and stories. When doing the newsletter monthly became too time consuming with her other school and music activities, Lauryl settled into a quarterly schedule and has kept the newsletter going for over three years. During that time, *Sisters* evolved into a newsletter primarily for home schooled teenagers around the country, and with herself as editor/publisher and a staff of six, the subscriber list continues to grow.

Jenny, another young writer I know, and her mom composed their family newsletter on their computer, and then with a click of the Send button, E-mailed the *Cutler Courier* to twelve relatives across the miles including grandparents, two college cousins, aunts, and uncles.

Each of these young people have discovered the fun of writing newsletters. Kids can develop good journalism skills when they interview people and gather news, besides all the practice they get doing informative writing. They have an interested audience to write for—a key ingredient in the writing process. They also get feedback from their readers in the form of an occasional phone call or note saying how much they enjoy getting the newsletter.

Helping your child start a newsletter is a great way to keep in touch with relatives and friends across the country and around the globe. Although your family or neighborhood news won't usually make the network news, it's important to those who read it.

Writing bonds families. Family ties are strengthened, bridges built between the old and young generations, and kids feel a sense of belonging as they experience a stronger connection to their extended family members.

You never know where the family newsletter will go once you get it started. I know of family newsletters that have been going on for more than fifty years. If you and your child get the ball rolling, your family newsletter may make it into the twenty-first century.

Writing the Newsletter: How to Get Started

Writing a family newsletter is easy and lots of fun. It could be as simple as two pages of news about baby brother's new teeth and first steps, the family vacation, and a birthday party, written in longhand and illustrated by your seven-year-old. The newsletter could be a joint project written on the computer by all of your children. Your help depends on the age of your child and her writing skills and interest level. With a little encouragement and assistance in the first steps, she may take off and enjoy the new role of editor.

Here's how to get started:

• Get together with a few family members and brainstorm possible titles for your own newsletter. You could have a contest: Let each person submit ideas for the name and vote on the favorite one.

• Have your artistic child design a logo or print in fancy or plain letters the masthead of the newsletter. Here's the current masthead for our family's newsletter:

Heath Herald
Spring Newsletter

• Help your child come up with a preliminary letter and little survey to send out to family members asking questions like:

1. What's happening in your neck of the woods? What's your NEWS FLASH item? _____
_____

2. My favorite movie I've seen or book I've read lately that I could recommend: _____
_____

3. What's happening in school and/or sports:
_____
_____

4. Our birthdays are: (List)
5. Our fax # or E-mail address is:

Other questions you might ask encourage family members to share about awards, anniversaries, humor, college news, new job information, weddings, graduations, relocations, favorite foods or family recipes, etc. Of course you can adapt the questions if you're doing a neighborhood newsletter or one for a circle of friends.

Enclose the survey with a cover letter. Here's a sample of one I wrote when I started our family newsletter about eight years ago.

Dear Family,

I'm starting a newsletter entitled *Heath Herald* so we can all stay better connected and "in touch" between our yearly reunion since everyone is so busy. I'm writing to ask you to participate. Here are some "columns" or sections I hope to cover in our newsletter: FAMILY TRIVIA AND BREAKING NEWS, PET PORTIONS (news about our canine and feline pals), SCHOOL DAYS (what your kids are doing in school), ATHLETES IN ACTION. I'd also like to include old family sayings, recipes, and special events from time to time. If you have information on any of these topics, please send it to me for our first issue. If you want to help in any other way or have an idea for another column—great! You can write it.

Please write or call me with your news by June 15. Thanks!

Learning along the Way

I've learned a lot since that very first issue of *Heath Herald*. When I started our family newsletter, I enlisted not only my own children, but also the young writers in the extended family. It was a year or so after my mother died and I could see that, without the hub of the family keeping us all informed and in touch, my five siblings and I and our children were getting disconnected. I decided to do something about it—and the newsletter worked. We send out the four- to five-page newsletter four times a year.

We find it works best to rotate editorship (but I attempt to keep the ball rolling by awarding budding family writers a guest editorship), and even the younger cousins get involved in being their side of the family's editor and gathering and reporting news. We include that season's birthdays and anniversaries to jog memories so cards can be sent and congratulations offered.

The newsletter has been a big hit and is especially appreciated by college cousins who are 1,000 miles away at a university or those who've recently moved. I try to include something about each family member—youngest to oldest—as these samples show:

> **Wynne Leslie** enjoys life in downtown Chicago. She and beau **James** find time between long hours of work at their restaurants to picnic along Lake Michigan, go to a festival or symphony. They were engaged Labor Day weekend and plan a May or June wedding. Wynne hopes everyone can come!
>
> **Eve**, in the llth grade, is enjoying a course in meterology, is an avid reader, and is at the top of her Ponder High School class. She is undergoing a five-week round of chemotherapy to arrest her juvenile rheumatoid arthritis. She enjoyed her trip to Oklahoma City to spend a weekend with Aunt Cheri.

Even the pets are included:

> **Jet**, George and LouAnn's black puma-cat, is the hunter of the family. She still faithfully presents her family with small prey she

traps and disposes of herself. She is baffled these days by the realistic bird sounds made by their new encyclopedia computer program, which the boys play to tease her.

We announce the next Heath reunion or gathering, include some trivia or a family history story, and are always open to new ideas for the newsletter.

A Little Help to Get Started

If your child gets excited about the idea, you could supply paper and pens, and a computer if possible. There's lots of desktop publishing software that makes creating a professional-looking newsletter with graphics an easy, fun process. A computer is not essential, however. Handwritten and illustrated newsletters are quite charming. The frequency and method is up to you and your kids. You could try a Christmas newsletter once a year or do one more often.

Try tackling this project together, sharing your own family news, and you'll be amazed at how your children's writing skills and family ties will strengthen.

Writing a Neighborhood Newspaper

Suggest your child gather a few friends and start their own neighborhood gazette. It's a perfect summer project. There are so many things to do to write and publish a newspaper that there are plenty of jobs to go around for each friend who wants to be involved.

The editor takes care of the overall managing of the newspaper. The editor assigns, coordinates, and reviews articles and columns. The editor would make sure each article covers the *who, what, where, when,* and *how* of each event or feature.

Reporters can be as numerous as you have interested kids. Reporters interview neighbors, gather news, and write the articles. For instance, one reporter could write an article about the Christmas community yard sale coming up. Another could interview the new kid on the block and write a story about him and where his family came from. Everyone on the staff can brainstorm on ideas for future articles.

The *art director* lays out the articles and photos into the newspaper pages and may draw a cartoon, comic strip, or add other art to the paper.

The *advertising director* gets a few local businesses (or parents) to buy ad space. Families who want to advertise garage sales are good possibilities for advertising space.

You could also have someone in charge of printing who copies the newspaper at mom's business or a local copy shop, a subscription manager who sells the newspaper to families, friends, and interested neighbors to cover the cost of production, and columnists who write a regular column on a topic like sports, community issues, or school news.

Other features could include: an advice column, book or movie reviews, a page to showcase original writing and art by neighborhood kids, and community classifieds where equipment, toys, and pets for sale could be listed.

What a great project for energetic neighborhood friends! Besides getting some terrific writing practice, children involved in publishing a newspaper receive some terrific business experience.

Exercises

1. After your family has come back from an outing or trip (e.g. zoo, circus, state fair, etc.), let your child write about the experience as if he were a reporter for a family newspaper.

2. Look at a local or regional newspaper with your child and talk about the features: masthead, comics, sports section, etc.

3. Look for news occurring right under your nose in the neighborhood or family and have your child interview the person involved and write a short feature story that answers the questions *who, what, when, where,* and *how* about the event or incident.

CHAPTER 9

Help, Mom! I've Got to Write a Book Report

*The child who is exposed naturally,
as part of a happy home life, to the work
of good writers, is fortunate indeed.*
—Frank Eyre

James runs into the kitchen and throws his backpack on the kitchen table. Grabbing his basketball off the floor, he heads for the driveway, and slams the door behind him.

"Not so fast!" Cynthia calls after him. "What homework do you have?"

"Not much," James replies. "Just a big book report due in two weeks. I hate book reports!"

James isn't alone. To many kids, a book report sounds like a boring exercise. They have to do it. They don't enjoy it. The teacher has to grade it. And often the parent ends up "helping" write the book report the night before it's due. How can your child write a book report that deserves an *A* grade but also is fun and interesting to write (and ready on time without *your* writing it)?

Choosing a Book and Reading It

Book selection is crucial. The book has to be *read* before the report can be written. If the book isn't read, the book report is a nightmare for student, parent, and teacher. You'd be surprised at the number of kids who throw the assigned book in their lockers and never read it. Then either the student fabricates the book report or cheats off of another student's work. "The kids who have the most trouble writing book reports are the students who didn't read the books or they read the first few pages and then ditched it," said Marilyn Morgan, a veteran sixth grade teacher in Dallas, Texas. Watching the movie version of the book or using one of the study guides/summaries does not replace reading the book.

However, if a book captures your child's attention and he gets hooked on reading it, the book reporting process will go much smoother. Here are some tips on selecting a book. (You should first check to see if a book has to be pre-approved by the teacher or if there is a book list to chose from.)

• *Have your child write down a short list of his favorite authors and books.* Sometimes choosing a book by a favorite, familiar author is a sure way to motivate a reader. If your daughter enjoyed one of Dian Regan's juvenile mysteries, for example, she's likely to enjoy Dian's next book. Writers of books for young readers frequently work in series of books.

• *Fiction or nonfiction?* What kind of book does your child enjoy the most? Brainstorm and jot down his ideas on his favorite type of book: science fiction, time travel, biography and autobiography, adventure/action, historical fiction, mysteries.

• *What are your child's interests?* When Tommy's seventh grade teacher realized his passion was motorcycles, she found a book with a main character riding across the United States on a motorcycle. Not only did he finish the novel, but his book report was his best piece of writing all year. Tap into your child's center of learning excitement and the book report will be better and easier to write. It's not hard to write about something you're excited about.

Go to a bookstore together and get someone to suggest books he might enjoy. A bookstore that caters to children or that has a special children's section is best. The staff love books and they've read many of them and describe them with enthusiasm. They can dialogue with your child, help choose a book, and pique his interest. In the same way, a librarian at the public library can also quickly zero in on a good book for your child.

Sometimes the teacher assigns a book and the student has no choice. Here are some ways to make the reader's experience a bit more enjoyable.

• *Choose a cozy corner.* When the book comes home, encourage your child to choose a comfortable place to read in. A beanbag chair, big pillows on the floor, a makeshift tent constructed with a card table covered by a sheet for the younger child all make good reading spots. Kids are more likely to read when they have a place to sprawl out or curl up on.

• *Break the book into small chunks.* Help your child pace her reading. Divide the number of pages into the days left until the report is due. Then subtract a few days (for the writing process), and you'll have a round number of pages that she'll need to read per day or week in order to finish the book report on time. Write this on a calendar and make it part of every day's homework. Reading a whole 150- to 200-page book may sound and look overwhelming, but when you break the reading down into manageable chunks, your child can rise to the challenge. It's also great practice in organization and builds time management skills.

• *Read together.* If you have a younger child or a reluctant reader, you might read the first few chapters aloud together to help him get started until interest builds. You can read a paragraph or page and your child can then read a corresponding section, while you both discuss the content or illustrations along the way. After a chapter or two of reading a high-interest book aloud, your child will likely take off and want to get to the next episode. When that happens, you can step back.

• *Have a SSR (silent sustained reading) time* for thirty minutes after dinner, in which television and music is turned off. Each family member reads something silently for the specified amount of time (and your child reads her book).

• *Reward your child* for meeting reading goals. When she's halfway through the book, take her out for a frozen yogurt. When she has completed the book, take an outing to a bookstore and let her choose a new kids' magazine or book.

Get Organized

Once the book is read, it's time to get organized. This is where parents can help the most—by discussing and helping kids make an informal outline or notes. Then, instead of staring at a blank piece of paper, the book report writer will have notes to springboard from. There are several ways to help while not taking over the project.

Talk about the book first. For most kids, discussion is a terrific aid in the prewriting process. Often teachers just don't have the class time to discuss each book, especially if individual books are read instead of a class-assigned book. But discussion and focused questions help the writer think, organize his thoughts and formulate opinions. You could say to your child, "I'm going to interview you just like a reporter, and take notes." Then write down everything your child says, in his own words, and he'll have some handy notes to work from. Ask questions using the five *W*'s and the *H*:

• Why did you choose this book?
• Where does this story take place?
• What is the book about?
• What do you think the author's main idea was in writing the book?
• What was the most interesting (or funny, or sad, depending on the content) part of the whole book to you?
• How does the book end?

Even if your child didn't like how the main character reacted or hates the ending, you have a good angle for discussion. You could ask, "What would you do if you were that character?" or "If you could write a different ending, what would it be?"

As he talks and discussion continues, write down what he says. Be a sounding board and listener rather than giving all the answers. Discussing the book in this way works really well for the child who has read the book but has writer's block or freezes up when it's time to write the report. No matter what kind of book report is assigned, talking over questions like those listed above will help your child process the book's content and boost critical thinking skills and comprehension.

Provide sentence starters. Cues can jump-start your child's memory after reading a long book that he started several weeks before the writing. Jot down a few sentence starters and let him finish the sentences:

- My favorite character in the book is . . .
- The story took place in . . .
- The most exciting part of the book is . . .
- My favorite chapter is . . .
- The theme (or main idea) this story gets across to the reader is . . .

Then over breakfast or while driving in the car, talk over his responses. Discussing your child's responses can help him process the content, characters, and plot of the book, enabling him to be ready to write the book report.

Know the teacher's expectations for the book report. "Perhaps the most important thing for parents to know is what's required in the book report," says Janet Martin, an Eagle Nest, New Mexico, middle school writing teacher. Find out exactly the components she wants. For example, has the teacher given questions to be answered in the body of the report, such as "What is the turning point in the plot?" "What is the climax of the story?" "What conflict is central to the story and how is it resolved?" "Who is the main character and how does he/she change from the beginning to the end of the story?" Or has the teacher assigned an essay to write (e.g., an essay explaining the thesis or theme underlying the story, or how you would change the ending of the story)? Does the teacher plan for the book reports to be read aloud to the class? What is her focus in the assignment?

Whatever your child's age, if you really want to spark his reading and book report writing, try the Parents Sharing Books approach developed at Indiana University's Family Literacy Center. The director, Carl Smith's son Tony was an active thirteen-year-old who didn't like reading or homework, but when Tony was small, he would stand in the yard at night fascinated with the stars. Though curious about astronomy and space, in school he made *C*'s and *D*'s. He was breaking curfew, getting in a bit of trouble, and wasn't communicating with his parents.

One day Tony's teacher recommended a science fiction book called *Dune*, about a group of people who lived on a desert planet. For the first time in a long time, Tony was excited about something assigned at school and he told his dad about the book. His father, Carl, seized the opportunity to go out and get the paperback to read it at the same time so he and Tony could discuss the story at dinnertime. Their relationship began to change as they shared their opinions and went on to read other books. Tony's attitude, behavior, and even his grades improved, and he continued to talk to his dad about things he wouldn't have discussed previously because the book talks were a kind of bridge. Thousands of parents around the country have used this approach with great success.

Creative Book Reporting

Perhaps the teacher gives options or accepts a creative approach to book reporting. If you're home schooling your child, you can choose the book report format yourself. In that case, one of these ideas can spark the imagination and help get children hooked on books. Sometimes extra credit can be given for a project that accompanies a standard book report.

• *Write the book from a different point of view.* Take an entire story or a chapter and write a version from a different character's point of view. For example, the third pig in *Three Little Pigs* might say, "I told my brothers that straw and sticks just wouldn't do. Those are not enough protection from a hungry wolf. Now me, I'm using bricks!"

• *Write the diary a main character might have written.* Imagine you are the person in your book and write a diary for a few days or weeks just like you think he or she would have written it.

• *Write an advertising campaign for a movie about the book.* This could even include newspaper ad layouts, radio and television commercials, and announcements about any special events.

• *Write a letter to the author of the book.* Discuss how the author's book impacted you and why you recommended it to your friends, why you think he or she is one of the best children's authors, or why you would read other books of his. Send the letter to the author in care of the book publisher. Your child might just receive a personal reply.

• *Convert the book to a radio drama script, a television series episode, or a puppet show script.* Then perform a live or taped version of the story, or a scene from the book—as a radio play or a made-for-television movie. Include an announcer and sound effects.

• *Transform the events of the story into a ballad or song.* Write the lyrics and music and perform it for the family or class.

• *Impersonate a character and tell an episode in a book.* Dress up as a character from the book and retell the story. Use props and write notes on index cards to aid your presentation. Or impersonate the author and come to visit the class who in turn interviews him or her.[1]

Writing about Books

Literature can provide excellent reasons to write, and the reader's response to a book can be a paper written on it. Here are some good topics to write about a book.

• Compare and contrast two books by this author that you've read. How are they alike and how are they different? From reading

[1] Adapted from *Fifty-five Ways to Respond to a Book*, by Mrs. Posy Lough, Simsbury, Connecticut, a former teacher and president of the Posy Collection.

these two books, what kind of person do you think the author is? What does he like and care about? What have you observed about him as a writer?

• If you could spend the day with a character from the book, which character would you choose and why? Plan an itinerary for that day telling where you would go and how you would spend the time.

• If you could ask the author one question about this book, what would it be?

• How do you think this book can help you or other children?

• Imagine you are a newspaper reporter. Write a news or feature article on the most important event in the book you've read.

Making a Book Quilt

Making a book quilt or wall hanging is an ideal project for a home school parent or a classroom if you have any basic sewing or quilting skills. It's great for kids who need a hands-on approach to learn best and for children who love painting and drawing.

After completing the reading of a book, give each child a 9" × 9" or smaller square of muslin. Then brainstorm on all the different scenes in the book. Have each child take a different scene and, using crayons, draw a scene on his square and color all the figures in. Puffy Paint works well to outline and add color and texture to the quilt squares. You can add a square for each main character, a square for the title, and one for a memorable quote from the book. After the muslin squares are drawn and the figures colored in, put a piece of white typing paper over and under the square and iron each one to set the color. Sew all the blocks together and add a three-inch border of solid-colored material. Use yarn or heavy string or thread to tie a knot at each corner of the squares and secure the quilt. If you just have one child, he could make a three-paneled wall hanging and draw three scenes on muslin, or make a pillow out of just one square. These story quilts are a wonderful learning tool and fun to hang and display on the wall.

With a good selection of a book and some discussion and preparation, book reporting may become one of your child's favorite academic assignments. Once your child has written an effective book report and experiences some success, you'll be rewarded with the lack of procrastination and groaning the next time one is assigned. Reading a book and knowing how to discuss the content is one of the important basics of learning and will yield dividends throughout your child's education.

Exercises

1. A fun way to write about a book and create a card catalogue for your own library is to give your child a set of recipe cards (3" × 5" index cards work well, too) and have him write a recipe describing the most delicious parts of the book. Be sure the book's author and title appear on the recipe. After proofreading, have your child copy the completed recipes on colorful recipe cards and store them in a small file box near your family library to help other family members select a good book.

2. To help your child become a more well-rounded reader, play Book Bingo. Get an 8½ " × 11" sheet of paper and make a bingo grid with *BOOKS* written across the top in squares and under it, five squares across and five down (see below for example). In each square, put different kinds of books your child could read such as *Mystery, Historical Fiction, Sports, Biography, Science Fiction*, etc. Then, when it is time to pick a book, he finds a different kind on the grid and after the book is read, you put a star or sticker over that square. When a bingo occurs (a row of stars horizontally, vertically, or diagonally), provide a treat (like a coupon for a new book at the bookstore or something related to your child's favorite interest).

Name:

B	O	O	K	S
Mystery	Science Fiction	Historical Fiction	Free Choice	Realistic Fiction
Realistic Fiction	Fantasy Fiction	Animals	Science or Fantasy Fiction	Free Choice
Animals	Free Choice	Mystery	Realistic Fiction	Historical Fiction
Science Fiction	Sports	Realistic Fiction	Animals	Mystery
Free Choice	Realistic Fiction	Historical Fiction	Sports	Biography

Creative Journal Keeping: The Best Practice for Developing Writers

Ideas are like rabbits. You get a couple and learn how to handle them and pretty soon you have a dozen.
—John Steinbeck

Kids have terrific ideas. Childhood is the most creative time of life, and if children's ideas are jotted down in a notebook or journal, they aren't lost; in fact, they generate more ideas.

There are lots of reasons to encourage our children to write in journals: the regular writing practice improves language skills, a journal is a great vent for anger and mixed emotions (kids, like adults, have plenty of those), and it provides a way for children to focus and clarify their thoughts and opinions. In addition, writers develop their own voices and styles by regularly writing in a journal. Kids can write about anything in their journals and aren't restricted to an assignment as they are in school. A child experiences self-discovery as she writes; she actually begins to understand what she's thinking by writing it down. As Anne Frank, one of the most famous young journal writers said, "Paper is more patient than man."

Many famous writers throughout history have kept journals. A study of Newbery Award–winning authors showed that one thing they all had in common is that they wrote in journals in their child-hood and as they were growing up.

How do you get your child to begin writing in a journal? Posy and

Tom, Connecticut parents, had both enjoyed journaling in their own lives growing up, so they wanted their son, Kyser, to keep a journal. They gave him a number of little spiral notebooks that fit in his pocket and encouraged him to jot down his observations of things when he went on family field trips, school outings, and even in his backyard exploring. Kyser saw his dad write notes on 3" x 5" cards he always kept in his pocket, and he began to imitate this journaling. Now, at twelve years old, he's a regular journal keeper. When he and his dad went to the Olympics in Atlanta, Kyser took along his pocket notebook. When they traveled to New Hampshire, he wrote down observations of what he saw and experienced on a hike and at a museum.

Brooke, a college student, remembered that her journaling began when, at the age of twelve, she found a journal her mother had written when she was twelve years old. Brooke enjoyed reading her mother's journal so much she thought, "If I start writing now, maybe my daughter can read what life was like growing up in Oklahoma in the '80s and '90s." Through her adolescent years she wrote poems, prayers, thoughts, stories, descriptions of her favorite books, and dreams for her future, and she's still writing journals in college.

Even kindergartners who are just barely learning to read can write in a journal when we give them their own special book. They can dictate ideas and stories for parents to write down, draw pictures, and write in invented spelling just for the fun of it. A brightly colored folder with pockets and filled with both blank and lined paper makes a good journal for a child.

Writing on the Road

One summer when our family took a trip to Washington, D.C., and Maine, I gave our three children each a cloth-bound blank book and told them our goal was to write once a day about the highlight of that particular day of travel. With a 4,000 mile journey ahead in the car, I figured they would have plenty of time to write. We took along car games, books on cassette tape, and other stuff to entertain them, but the journals were a hit. Here are some excerpts from their travel journals:

> Today I went to the Smithsonian Natural History Museum and saw the hugest dinosaurs. I was able to get a wheelchair since I'd had an appendectomy before we left, and Justin wheeled me around to look at everything. It was fun but a lot of people stared at me!
>
> —Chris, age 13

> Everywhere you look in Virginia, a picture could be painted— the rolling green valleys, masses of roadside trees—much more than Oklahoma, perfectly planted rows of corn. The other night we went to Alexandria, Old Town. It was very picturesque—the jointed townhouses, little knick-knack shops. There was lots of activity: crowds, lights, noise, cars, and street people wanting some money.
>
> —Justin, age 15

> On Lake Pennesseewassee in Norway, Maine, I learned to water-ski today. It was my favorite thing of the whole trip. I tried three times before I could get up on the skis and then went the whole way around the lake on skis! It felt unbelievable when I got up. The water was cool. I loved the speed!
>
> —Alison, age 10

Now that they are grown up, one married and two in college, these journals are a treasure. Here are some things I learned in the process to help motivate travel writing:

• Before the trip, go to a store and let your child pick out a journal that he or she would like to write in: a cloth-covered or spiral notebook of any color with lined or unlined paper (most children prefer lined paper). The journal could be a colored folder with pockets and notebook paper inside, which the child decorates to be his very own.

• Encourage writing daily on the trip, even if only for five minutes.

• Keep the journal accessible, not under mounds of suitcases in the back of the car where it will be hard to find.

• Encourage your child to write only the most special or favorite thing he did, ate, or experienced that day. It's not a diary listing every meal and activity of the day (that would become burdensome quickly). Instead, ask, "What was the strangest animal you saw today at the zoo? Describe it."

• Encourage your young writer to glue in postcards found along the way, a brightly colored leaf, menu or mementoes, photos and drawings.

If he's enjoyed the travel writing, encourage your child to continue journaling about the first day of school and experiences at home and at school.

Creating a Journal

A journal is a record of your child's experiences, his impressions and ideas, his hopes and dreams. I share with children when doing a writer's workshop that keeping a journal is like gardening: you plant the seed when you write down words and ideas. You water the seeds as you write more and revise some of the best. You fertilize the seeds as you share or read aloud something you've written. Like fruit and flowers, stories and poems will grow for you and others to enjoy.

Here are some tips to share with your young author to facilitate journal writing.

• Try to write in the journal daily, but don't feel bad if you don't have time. Just go back to writing in your journal the next day. It's just like playing a musical instrument or working out in gymnastics: you get better as you practice. If you carry the journal with you during the day, you'll find time to write—on the bus on the way to school or in the cafeteria after you've finished your lunch. You could write five to ten minutes before bed or early in the morning if you're an early bird.

• Give your journal your own title to make it personal like: *Jenny's Jottings, Mary's Musings*, or *Blake's Best Idea Notebook*. Have some stickers handy so you can jazz up the pages when you write and add anything creative (drawings, magazine clippings) that would make the journal uniquely your own.

• Date each entry. That way, when days or months have passed, you can look back and tell when you wrote something.

• Write quickly and don't worry about revising. Explore different kinds of writing as the ideas below suggest. Experiment and have fun.

• Find a private place to put the journal. And parents, make sure your children know their journal is off limits to other family members—no peeking! That way, your child can know that his private thoughts are kept that way unless he wants to share them with someone. You can let him know you'd love to hear a story or poem from the journal at dinnertime once in a while.

What Can I Write?

What kinds of things can children write in their journals? I like to give kids the following list of ideas for those times when they are having a hard time getting their thoughts down onto paper.

• *Quotations*: She can collect quotations that inspire her or that she finds thought provoking. These can be found on billboards, bumper stickers, in books, and in magazines. Your child can write it in her journal or if it's from a magazine, cut it out, glue it in the journal, and jot down thoughts on the quote or why she likes it.

• *Happy stuff*: Have your child make a list of things she loves or that make her happy: Christmas twinkle lights, a litter of new baby kittens, her red and purple kite. She can write about things she's grateful for or blessings she's glad about.

• *Hopes and dreams*: Writing a few lines on "When I grow up I want to be . . . and here's why. . . ." or "If I had two wishes, here's what they'd be . . ." or "If I was in charge of America, this is what I'd change . . ." inspires kids to develop hopes and dreams for the future.

• A wonderful thing to write in a journal is *Images of the Day*. Encourage your child to take a little time to notice sounds and interesting objects, tastes, and smells in everyday life. Have her notice the squealing sirens in the distance, the incessant barking of the dog when she's trying to sleep, the feel of the rough concrete beneath her bare feet—then write these images down. They don't have to be in complete sentences. Here's what Carrie wrote: "Airy bubbles cracking in my hot bathtub water, my brother stretched out on the brown carpet devouring chocolate ice cream, piles and piles of homework I need to do . . ."

• *An opinion of a movie or book:* Whether it's an old video of *E.T.* or a new movie, have your child write a few sentences telling someone why he should or should not see this movie and who his favorite character was.

• *Questions about anything:* Whatever she wonders about, is curious about, or would like to ask someone, she should write it down. Then encourage her to try to find an answer.

• *Poems:* Whether it is a simile, a four-line or a four-stanza verse, poetry sparks the imagination. It can be rhymed or unrhymed, silly or serious. See chapter 15 for lots of ideas on making poems.

• *Have your child list ideas of projects she'd like to do, things she'd like to learn, places she'd like to go,* such as a family field trip to the Smithsonian museum, or to take a pottery class, or to learn how to knit.

• *Pencil or pen sketches:* Doodles, cartoons, and drawings make a journal uniquely her own. She can also add stickers, newspaper clippings, cut-out words from ads, or photographs that might provide an idea to write about someday.

She can draw how she is feeling—sad, happy, frustrated, or a tangle of emotions. She can draw a self-portrait or a picture of her best friend and then write about him or her.

• *Favorites and unfavorites:* Encourage your child to write about her favorite kind of dog, favorite food, color, activity to do with friends (or unfavorites). Ask, "What do you like or dislike about school, or about being your age," etc.

Writing Descriptive "Showing" Paragraphs

The best writing shows instead of tells the reader about the action or what the characters in a story experience by using the five senses. Young writers need lots of practice showing instead of telling, and the journal is a good place to experiment.

Here's how: Using one of the sentences below (or one you make up), have your child write a descriptive paragraph about the topic, but he can't include the sentence in his writing. This kind of writing is a little like the game Charades: try to get the idea of the sentence across without telling the reader what it is. In other words, have your child try to convince the reader that the pizza tasted great or that his room is a messy disaster without writing "The pizza tasted great" or "My room is a messy disaster." Encourage your child to give details of sights, sounds, smells, textures, and tastes. Have him paint a picture with words.

Here are some sample sentences to play with:

- The cafeteria food was horrible.
- My hamburger was delicious.
- My room was so messy!
- My brother (sister) acted like a brat.
- The roller coaster ride was the scariest ride at the amusement park.
- Mom (or Dad) was angry!
- I was so embarrassed!
- He was a spy.
- The house was haunted.
- The boy (or girl) was terrified.

Here's how Kassie, one young writer wrote a showing paragraph of the sentence, "My room was so messy!"

After We Moved In

Boxes, packed and unpacked, were all over my room. I could hardly move. We had just moved into our new house. School had started and everything was disorganized. My clothes stuck halfway in my drawers and halfway out. My posters were all rolled up against my wall. Piles of butcher paper my breakables had been wrapped in were scattered everywhere. My clothes that were supposed to be hung in the closet were lying on my bed, still on the hangers. There were at least two glasses on my dresser with something in them that I'd been drinking while we moved in.

Here's how Leo, ten years old, wrote a showing paragraph of the sentence, "The concert was fantastic."

The smoke rose and three singers popped out on the stage. They started singing and wailing, and then one of them started smashing his guitar on the stage. Pieces of it went flying in every direction. The drummer poked his drumsticks into the drums, and people started fainting. They started throwing microphones. One went through the light near me. Sparks went everywhere. Boy, did we have fun!

Write Recollections

Encourage your child to write about a memory. Give her these directions:

Close your eyes and think as far back as you can. What picture comes to mind? A special Christmas? The birth of your baby sister? A big surprise your parents brought home to you? Write about it. Think about the first house you can remember living in. What happened there that you remember? Was it a birthday party, or the time you fell off your new bike in the driveway?

Our memories are storehouses of wonderful pieces of writing.

When we use our memory as a resource, lots of ideas for stories emerge, as this recollection shows.

The Seven-Year-Old Driver

One day, my sister and I were playing in the car. Allyson, my sister, was in the driver's seat and I was in the passenger seat. Allyson was pretending she was driving. I had my door open when Allyson pulled down the gear shift and we started rolling backward. I got really scared and jumped out! Allyson kept rolling backward in the car. She went down the driveway, across the street, and over a curb, almost hitting a tree! By the time Mom had gotten Allyson, I had dashed into the house and was on the couch. The car had slowed down when it hit the curb and Mom had gotten Allyson out of the car. Afterward, Mom gave us a lecture!

—Andrea Gesell

Another way to write a memory is to go to the spice rack or medicine cabinet, open the caps of the bottles, and let your child smell each one with her eyes closed. Does a particular smell remind her of Thanksgiving at Grandma's house? Does another aroma bring back a cold morning when you all sat around the table and had hot cocoa and cinnamon toast? Have your child write her memories down quickly, not worrying about errors or punctuation.

Freewriting in Journals

Freewriting means the writer just sits down, pen or pencil in hand, and writes for a specified amount of time—five or ten minutes—about anything that comes to mind or about a specific topic. It's amazing what happens when we get our thoughts and ideas out on paper through freewriting. We actually find out what we're thinking by writing it.

Have your child try this freewriting exercise: Give her a choice of words such as *rain, soccer, friends,* and *school* and suggest she freewrite for three to five minutes on one topic while you set a timer. Tell her to keep the pen moving until the timer rings, even if it means writing, "I can't think of anything to write." Tell her not to correct or edit her words or worry about what's going down on paper. Just get it down. Without stopping, let the words flow; write whatever comes out.

After your child has freewritten on one of the topics, ask if she'd like to read aloud what she's written. What this freewriting exercise shows is that words bring more words. Encourage her to use freewriting often in her journal. Offer the following suggestions.

• Get a recent incident, object, person, or scene that you've been involved with in your mind's eye. While you hold it there, begin to write.

• Freewrite about an emotion you've felt strongly—fear, jealousy, joy—or whatever is on your mind.

• Avoid stopping to revise or fix mistakes, and don't worry about picking exactly the right word. Editing is an important part of the writing process as we discussed in chapter 5, but it comes *after* the essential ideas of the poem or story are down on paper.

• After looking over a few of the freewriting exercises you've done in your journal, ask yourself, "What do I have?" It might be the seed of a personal experience story or the beginnings of a poem. Pick out the best part of what you wrote and develop that idea. See where it takes you.

FOCUSED FREEWRITING

Here are some topics you can suggest to your child that lend themselves to freewriting in journals.

• If our house caught fire and I could save only two objects, I would save _____ and _____ because . . .

• If I could spend an hour with the president (or some other famous person of the present or past) I would tell him . . .

• If I received a gift of $10,000, I'd spend it on . . .

- The most important character trait for a friend of mine to have is . . .
- My very favorite holiday or time of year is _____ because . . .
- My favorite television program or movie of all time is . . .
- The most puzzling thing I want answered when I get to heaven is . . .
- In a twenty-four-hour period, my most favorite time of the day is . . .
- I really get upset when . . .
- What I want to do more than anything someday is . . .

All around us, things are waiting to be noticed and written about. Observing them and writing about them in a journal will not only sharpen your child's writing but enliven his life.

Exercises

1. Get a journal for your child and let her decorate the cover.

2. Set a time this week in which everyone in the family gathers and writes something for twenty minutes—a journal entry, a letter. Provide paper, pencils, and pens.

3. Read one of the most famous journals a child wrote, *Diary of Anne Frank*. Talk about how writing about her feelings and experiences helped Anne cope with the hardships and difficulties she faced.

Story Writing Exercises

*Anyone who survived childhood
has enough material to write
for the rest of his or her life.*
—Flannery O'Conner

One of the easiest and most enjoyable writing activities for a child is a personal narrative, also called a personal experience story. Children—and adults, too—write best about firsthand experiences. We all have different experiences in the story of our life—some are funny, some sad, some make us angry, and some make us feel warm and happy. Perhaps that's what makes writing about these personal stories vivid and interesting—because there's a lot of emotion.

Since all children have memorable mishaps and accidents (like a first fall off her bicycle or first stitches), a scar story is an easy personal narrative to try first. I've also found that children show a certain amount of pride when telling of their misadventures.

Here is a fun way to teach your child to write a scar story.

Prewriting the Story

I use a prewriting strategy called *mapping* to help kids travel back into their memory and gather stories and details before writing. Actually, mapping is not a new technique. It's as old as the craft of novel writing, and was used as far back as 1881. On a foggy, rainy day that year, Robert Louis Stevenson, while trying to entertain his thirteen-year-old stepson, painted a map of an imaginary island with his watercolors. Stevenson began telling his stepson stories of the island, and remarked that the island looked like a fat dragon standing up. He quickly played on that idea by adding names such as "Spyeglass Hill," and "Cape of Ye Woods."

That island map was a springboard to one of Stevenson's most famous books, *Treasure Island*. As the author looked at his map of the island, the characters of the book began to emerge there among imaginary woods as they ran about fighting and hunting treasure. The next thing he knew, the first chapter was flowing, and the book began to take shape.[1]

We can take a lot of the anxiety out of story writing and make it a fun, entertaining process for kids when we use the same mapping strategy that Robert Louis Stevenson used in the writing of *Treasure Island*. Mystery writers use this technique when they first draw a sketch of the haunted house where a murder takes place before writing chapter one. I've used it for the prewriting process with children of all ages, varying ability levels, and different learning styles, and the results are tremendous. Mapping and telling of the personal experiences first, before writing, helps the story flow once the pen is put to paper. Here's how I go about applying this method:

PRIMING THE PUMP

First, I draw a map or simple sketch of the first house I remember living in or a grade school I attended. At whatever places or rooms in the house (or outside in the yard) I remember a story happening, I make an X and tell the story: of the scorpion that stung me as I was kneeling on the floor playing paper dolls one night, of the stitches my little sister had to have when we were fighting over who was going to feed the dog some bones and I threw a rock that just happened to hit her in the head, etc.

---

[1] Carol Madigan and Ann Elwood, *Brainstorms & Thunderbolts: How Creative Genius Works*, NY: MacMillan Publishing Co., 1983, p. 30.

This is a simple exercise that should only take a few minutes, but it is important. Not only does it serve to illustrate what I want the children to do, it gets their imaginations working and helps their memories go back to their own experiences.

DRAWING THE MAP

Once kids hear my stories, they want to tell their own. Not yet! I give them a big piece of manila drawing paper or typing paper and ask them to map a place where they spent some time and remember well, where some things happened that jump out in their memories. It could be the house they live in now or their first house, Grandma's farm or a camp they attended every summer.

I discourage them from adding too much detail (the very artistic kids want to draw everything or create an architectural house plan), asking them to sketch the map rapidly and wherever something happened, put a big **X**.

One child drew the campsite where his family had camped out in the summer and drew an X where his two-year-old little sister got lost and later was found by the lake. He drew another X where he got a bee sting and another where he caught his first big fish. The child chose to write about catching the fish, but the map could be put away and used another time as a resource for additional story ideas.

REHEARSING THE NARRATIVE BY STORYTELLING

Once the maps are sketched, I encourage the authors to tell one of the stories from their maps. If you are working with one child, have her tell you the story. If you are working with several children, you can pair them up.

Make sure they include the five *W*'s and the *H* in their narration by asking them the following questions: "How old were you?" "Where, when, and why did the experience or scar story happen?" "Who was involved? What actually happened and what was the outcome?" While the child is orally telling the story, she is rehearsing it. Now it's time to write.

DRAFTING THE STORY

If children have had a chance to map the story and tell the story, then they are more than ready to write the story. They should do it right after the storytelling while the thoughts and memories are rolling.

Here's what you can say: "Just get it down. Write on every other line of the paper. Don't worry at this point about grammar or spelling, just write the whole story like you just told it." Encourage them to describe the scene with the five senses: What did it feel like? Where did it hurt? What did it sound like (when she fell off her bike, for instance) or look like (the gash, that is)? What about taste, colors, and smells? It helps to encourage the writer to use dialogue, too—anything to make the reader feel like he is there in the story.

If a title occurs to the writer, have her jot it at the top. If not, don't worry about the title—you can create one later. Some writers like to call their narrative "My Scar Story" or "My First Stitches" but others want something more individual like "Fourth Grade Fight" or "Ouch!"

If a child has a hard time starting, I give a starter sentence based on hearing his experience like, "When I was five years old and on a camping trip with my family one summer . . ." and then he takes off writing the story.

MOTIVATING WRITERS

I love to read a story written by a child in a prior class, like this one called "The Microwave Cat."

One hot summer day when I was about two years old, we were having some people over to our house for dinner. My uncle, aunt, and grandparents had joined us and we were outside in the yard. Somehow my cat got in the sprinkler and became wet. My uncle, who was a teenager, suggested I should warm her up in the microwave. So I did!

After putting my cat in the microwave, I set the dial for twenty seconds. Then I started it and we heard a loud *scream* and then I opened the microwave and there she was—almost bare! My poor cat had not a hair left on her body. But within a few months she grew back her hair and we got the microwave clean and everything was fine!

We then talk about how to add sensory detail to the stories. What did the poor cat smell like when Kristin opened the microwave door? It smelled like burnt toast. We add that after "not a hair on her body" and then look at each writer's story to see what can be added to help the reader experience the scar story. By that point, we've actually done the first stage of revising.

You may want to read with your child the book *Broken Arrow Boy* (Landmark Publishers) written by Adam Moore, a nine-year-old boy who had a major misadventure—he fell on an arrow at a Cub Scout day camp. *Broken Arrow Boy* tells the story of how Adam recovered and how he and his family dealt with his injuries. It's a terrific book that children love. The illustrations drawn by Adam and photographs taken during the ordeal add appeal to the fascinating story told with sensory detail and description. This book really encourages kids to make the most of writing their own scar stories.

REVISING CONTENT

Since all good writing is rewriting, I ask, "Is there any information you need to add so the reader can understand the story more clearly?" and "Did you describe what you saw, felt, heard, and smelled?" The student can read his story aloud, and we conference together, looking for gaps in the story.

Next, work on word choice by focusing on *vivid verbs*. Vivid verbs give the reader a clear picture of the action—like saying "he *leaped* across the stage" instead of "he *ran* across the stage." Have your child use a highlighter and mark every action verb in the story. Write *walk* or *run* on a chalkboard or on paper and then brainstorm together, listing all the ways a person *runs* (jog, trot, dash, race) or *walks* (strut, creep, mosey, slither). Then have the young writer change some of the verbs in the story to vivid verbs that give the reader a picture of the action—the more descriptive, the better.

EDITING THE STORY

After the story is written and revised, it's time for proofreading. Act as the editor and consult with the author, choosing a few grammar, punctuation, or sentence mechanics to look for. Reading the story aloud while looking at the paper works best. You can suggest corrections with questions, but let the author keep the pen in her hand. Then check spelling the same way, being aware of what grammar and spelling skills the child has so as not to red-mark and discourage his writing.

ILLUSTRATING THE STORY

Children enjoy drawing a picture to illustrate their stories. Provide pencils, crayons, markers, even watercolor paint, and let your child get artistic. The illustration can be a detailed, more focused version of their map, or it can be a scene from the story. Another idea is to mount the story on a larger piece of construction paper and have the child draw a decorative border.

SHARING THE STORY

One of the most rewarding parts of writing is sharing the finished product. There are many ways to share or publish the story if your child is interested:

- Have your child read the story at the dinner table.
- Copy the story and illustration at a local copy shop and send it to grandparents or a family member.
- Send the story to a local newspaper's children's column. If your local paper doesn't have such a column to encourage young writers, suggest it and offer to gather some children's writing for the first column. This type of column is a great way to get new subscriptions from families and schools.

• Tack the story on the family bulletin board or refrigerator for everyone to enjoy.

• If appropriate for the writer's guidelines of a magazine your child subscribes to, send it to a magazine. Youth publications such as *Boys' Life, Highlights for Children*, and many others publish children's stories.

• Let your child make a collection of personal stories in a blank or handmade book.

The personal experience story doesn't have to be the story of an accident or scar story, although that's a great place to start for most kids. It can be an everyday slice of life, a humorous incident ("My Most Embarrassing Day," "The Longest Ten Seconds of My Life"), an adventurous encounter in neighborhood play, or an event the whole family experienced. It's a short story centered around a single incident and can run from a single paragraph to several pages. Once young writers learn how to compose a personal experience story, they'll be eager to write another.

Rewriting Folktales

Let your child pick a favorite folktale or fairy tale and then tell it from a different character's point of view, with a different plot or ending, or with an updated, modern twist. The familiarity of the tale gives the young writer a base to work from and his imagination can soar, as Kameron's does in his "True Story of Snow White by Her Stepmother."

To start the story out, I think I'll tell you about what Snow White was really like. Snow White was a spoiled, bratty princess. She hated me. She disliked me so much that she tried to spoil her father's and my marriage.

Now, let's go to the magic mirror. It isn't true about the magic mirror. That's just junk Disney put in to make it sound better. What happened was I sat by the mirror and thought about what a nice person like me could do to make Snow White like me.

I came up with the idea that I would have my hunter take Snow White in the woods. I chose that because I knew she loved animals. I don't know where they got the idea that I wanted to have her killed.

The huntsman, however, hated Snow White. He was the one who wanted her killed. But I insisted that she wasn't to be harmed. Instead he killed a deer and brought me its heart and left her there.

When he brought me the heart, I thought it was hers, so I threw it against the mirror and it shattered.

Meanwhile, Snow White was alive and living with The Seven Dorks. I got their address and sent my maid to give her an apple. When the maid gave it to her, she was saying thank you so much that she hyperventilated. Then a prince came and did CPR because he thought she was dead.

The Seven Dorks were at their twenty-four-hour job. So Snow White ran off with the prince, and nobody ever saw her again.

Group Stories

Whether it's a group of children at your house for a sleepover or a family night activity, writing a group story facilitates spontaneous responses and creativity, gives kids support as they springboard off each others' ideas, and offers an audience to give feedback. The interaction is a boost to their language development and is just plain fun. Here are some ways to tell and write group stories.

• *Round-robin stories* are great story starters. Sit in a circle. One person begins the story with a sentence. The next person adds another sentence or two of action, or perhaps a new character, and then passes the story line to the next participant. Have one child act as the scribe and write down the story as it develops.

• *Instant tall tales*: Name three unrelated objects, such as a lion, a haystack, and an Oreo cookie, and tell these to the first person in the circle. Then have him make up and tell a short three- or four-minute story using these objects somewhere in his narrative. Then he tells the next child three objects and that person creates a story. Story-telling passes around to everyone in the circle. After telling the stories, they can be written down and illustrated.

• *Write a mystery.* Pass out clues that have been written on index cards, giving a few clues to each person in the group. Then they read their clues, arrange them in some kind of order and write a detective story or mystery.

• *Dramatic storytelling*: Gather some hats and costumes. Have each person pick a hat or costume and put it on, then make up a name for her character. Collaborate on acting out and then writing the story.

Exercises

1. After you have finished reading or telling a story to your child:

    • Let the child retell the story in her own words.
    • Let her write a new ending to the story.

2. Have your child make a map of someplace that lots of things happened—like first summer camp, Grandma's farm where he spent two weeks with his cousins last summer, or the first school or house he remembers. Then have him make a movie in his mind of the event and relate the story to you.

3. Have your child write the personal experience story to you after telling it, or if he's a prereader, he can dictate the story and you write it down. Encourage illustrating. Then share the story with someone.

4. Have your child write and illustrate her own version of a fairy tale such as:

> Hansel & Gretel
> The Three Bears
> Little Red Riding Hood
> Cinderella
> The Gingerbread Boy

CHAPTER 12

Bookmaking Projects for Children

If a book comes from the heart,
it will continue to reach other hearts;
all art and authorcraft are of small amount to that.
—*Thomas Carlyle*

Twenty-four wiggling but attentive seven-year-olds sat in a circle with me. All eyes were on Amy, who was sitting in the author's chair, eager to share her just-completed *Someday* book.

"This book is dedicated to my best friend, Tiffany," Amy announced, smiling as she showed the class her cover and dedication page. Covered with carefully drawn yellow and red butterflies and balloons, the book was the culmination of four weeks of our bookmaking workshops. Oohs and aahs echoed around the circle as her classmates responded, "That's a cool cover, Amy! Neat butterflies . . ." "Let me see your inside illustrations!" said another.

Amy began reading on page one: "Someday I'd like to win a big gymnastics competition and get to go to the Olympics."

Turning each page, she continued reading as all eyes watched her book. "Someday a delivery man will come to my door and say it is my birthday every day! Then I'll get every Barbie and toy in the world except boy stuff."

"Now it's time to get back to reality. It's time to start my life." Amy read her last page and then went on to share her About the

Author page and enjoy a lively round of applause. Then the next student took center stage to share his hardback book.

After writing and publishing their first book in the workshop, many of my students went on to produce numerous books at home on subjects as varied as their interests: soccer, science fiction, a potpourri of poems, and raising puppies.

The Bookmaking Process

Making books is worth the time and effort because it gives children the chance to see and participate in the whole process from beginning to end: the preparation and idea gathering, the mistakes and errors along the way, problem solving, planning the cover and illustrating, persevering, and producing the finished product. They are involving the whole writing process to make the book, too: prewriting, drafting, revising, editing, and publishing.

Along the way, they get experience and practice with all the essential communication skills of reading, writing, spelling, grammar, and punctuation. When I have done bookmaking projects with children, I've found that when given a chance to do real writing for a real audience, children entered into the process like real authors who take pride in their work. Even those I'd been warned were troublemakers or had attention problems were motivated by writing and illustrating their own book for the class collection in the library, which the whole school would get to read. Kids of different levels of ability could write marvelous books. And many kids insisted on coming in at recess to work on their books.

How to Write a *Someday* Book

A *Someday* book is an ideal book project for home school or classroom, especially for grades two through five. Children are afire with ideas and hopes for the future, even before middle school years, and writing a *Someday* book gives them an opportunity to think about and share their dreams. Here's how to get started:

• *Read the book* SOMEDAY, *by Charlotte Zolotow.* You can check out this children's book at a library or purchase it inexpensively at a bookstore. As you read with your child, talk about the illustrations, the different ways the word *someday* is written on each page, and how the title page, dedication, and other parts of the book are put together.

• *Talk about what your child would like to have happen someday.* Ask questions like, "What would you like to do when you grow up if you could do anything?" "What's a dream or goal you've always had?" "What kind of pet would you like to have?" "Where would you like to travel?" Record these on a *cluster* as you brainstorm together.

Brainstorming and clustering is a great technique for generating ideas; it's not intimidating, and once the creativity starts flowing, a great part of the work is done. Kids write things in their cluster like:

• Someday I will become president of the United States and stop all drugs.
• Someday I'll meet Michael Jordan and get to play basketball with him.
• Someday I will become a scientist and find a cure for cancer.
• Someday I'll come to school and my teacher will say, "You got all *A*'s!"
• Someday I'll meet Shannon Miller and become an Olympic gymnast.
• Someday I will be an astronaut and visit Mars.

The dreams and hopes don't have to be serious; they can be fanciful like wanting to fly around the world in a hot air balloon or "Someday I'll get a broom and it will turn into a sword and my house will turn into a castle, and my Dad would be Ganon, my sister Zelda, and I would be Link!"

• *Make a mock-up book first.* Fold six to ten sheets of blank white typing paper in half, and staple them to create pages for the book. Before stapling, put a bright piece of construction paper on the bottom for the cover. Have your child write the practice book in pencil so it can be easily edited.

• *Open out the pages and designate*: Write in pencil at the bottom of each page the page number:

Page 1: title page
Page 2: dedication
Page 3: first page of the text of the book
Last page: About the Author page

• *Start writing and illustrate each* Someday *page.* Here are some tips that smooth the writing process:

Use a pencil or erasable ballpoint pen for the writing, and water-based markers or colored pencils for the illustrations. You might suggest keeping both the cover and page illustrations simple. (For example, three balloons or one teddy bear with title and author on the cover works better than fifty butterflies.)

Make a guideline sheet to put under the blank page. Just take a piece of standard lined notebook paper and with a black marker, make a neat bold line over each line so that it will show through the book pages. Then your child can slip the guideline sheet under each page and write straight across without being frustrated by squiggling the lines up and down on the page.

When using pencils, have two on hand, sharpened and with clean erasers.

Ease the editing and revision process by sitting beside the author and having her read her book aloud. Decide on one aspect to revise, such as to improve word choice by making the verbs and nouns more vivid or expanding information and details. See chapter 5 on editing and grammar for suggestions. Then proofread the book together, looking for misspelled words, grammar errors, etc. The proofreading expectations need to be age-appropriate. Remember, the writer will stay more motivated if the pen—and thus owner-ship—stays in his hands and you provide the consulting and encouragement.

When the *Someday* book is complete, find ways to share it. The word *publishing* actually means *sharing*, and there are so many ways for your child to do that. You can take it over to Grandma's on your next visit so she can enjoy reading the book. The author can read it to a younger sibling or group of children. They love to read each oth-ers' writing and enjoy the illustrations. The school or public library can do a display of local young authors' books and stories. Look in the last chapter for more ways to publish and share.

More Bookmaking Ideas

Once kids have tasted the fun of bookmaking and gone through the process, they are often eager to write other kinds of books that express their interests. Books can be written and illustrated on all kinds of topics, both fiction and nonfiction. They can write an auto-biographical book, a sports story, a spy thriller, or historical fiction. The key is to link the subject matter of the book with something your child wants to learn more about, a favorite topic, or vital interest. Here are a few ideas:

How to Be a Top Baby-sitter
How to Breed Tropical Fish
My Book of Family History
Susan's Personal Glimpses (A Collection of Personal Experience
    Stories)
Rainbows and Dreams: A Poetry Collection
Star Trek in the Twenty-First Century

If you want a really professional-looking book, check with these companies where you can order white, hardback books (profession-ally bound) with blank pages for a low price:

Treetop Publishing
P.O. Box 85576
Racine, WI 53408-5567

Sundance Publishers
Newtown Road
Littleton, MA 01460

Let's Make a Cookbook

Creating a cookbook is an enjoyable parent-child activity that combines writing, art, and food—a winning combination. Here's how to get started:

• Get a spiral, unlined notebook (with heavy-gauge paper if possible). The art department of a discount store or hobby store is a good place to look.

• Gather some stamps with vegetable and fruit designs and colorful ink pads (child-safe are best) to print on the pages of the cookbook. Add some watercolors, colored pencils, or markers if your child would want to draw his or her own pictures of ingredients or finished food creations or color inside the stamped designs.

• Let your child write his or her favorite recipes, one on a page. The cookbook can have a seasonal theme, such as holiday recipes or summer treats. The title and cover illustration can reflect the theme. Decorate pages with the vegetable and fruit stamps as a border or under each recipe.

• Enjoy the finished cookbook at home where you can display it in the kitchen and then make and eat some of the recipes. Or wrap and tie a bright ribbon around the original cookbook and give it as a cherished gift to grandparents or a teacher.

A classroom can create a cookbook on computer, with each student supplying his or her favorite recipe. The information—type of food, ingredients needed, preparation, how good it tastes, who contributed, etc.—can be supplied by each child. All the recipes can be keyed into the computer, organized according to type of food, and printed out. Then the recipes can be glued into blank books and illustrated by the children.

ABC Books

Check out some ABC books at the library. There are some very creative alphabet books with wonderful illustrations. Many top illustrators and children's authors have written an ABC book—even Isaac Asimov, the science writer, and Brian Wildsmith, a noted artist and children's book illustrator. Read several alphabet books aloud together and enjoy the diversity of the books and the illustrations.

Then ask your child what he's most interested in: his passion, his biggest interest. This could be an NFL football team, aliens, guitar playing, planets, ballet, or even Superman comics. Pick out a subject just to demonstrate and with a chalkless board or big sheet of paper write the alphabet and leave room beside each letter. For example, if your subject is *The ABC Book of Animals*, start with *A* and write the word *alligator* next to the letter. For *B*, write the word *bird*. For *C*, *cheetah*. Continue brainstorming together through the alphabet for the best word for each letter.

With the blank book (see directions below to make one), let your child begin writing his ABC book. Encourage him to illustrate each alphabet letter (or he can use cut-out magazine pictures or photographs). Jennifer, a home schooling parent who has her kids make big books, uses a large sheet of poster board for each page. She encourages her children to not only make original drawings for each letter, but to use three-dimensional art. They have used all kinds of media to paint and illustrate their big books: watercolor, markers, and acrylics. When Benjamin got to the *K*, for example, he made a real kite and glued it to the page. He made a leaf rubbing and attached it to the *L* page. These ABC books can be as creative as your child wants to be.

When Posy Lough did ABC books with her sixth-grade class,

Ernest, a special education child, said, "I have the greatest idea! Could I go to the library so I can use the large dictionary?" After several days of work with the big dictionary, Ernest created a book he called *The Educated ABC Book*. For each letter of the alphabet he found the longest, most difficult word and wrote its definition and illustrated the word. Another child who loved fishing created *The ABC Book of Fishing*. When they heard him read his book, the class was astounded at how much he knew about fishing. Kids love making books about something they feel like an expert at. And they often go on to write the *ABC Book of My Mother*, to give for Mother's Day or *The ABC Book of Christmas*.

You can use this book idea with family trips. When you go to a new state, a science or history museum, or a special outing to the ocean, have your child look for something for each letter of the alphabet and jot it on a piece of paper. When he gets back in the car (if it's a long trip) or home, he can write each letter in the blank book and design a cover. On the pages for some of the illustrations he can use postcards or things found along the journey. The *ABC Book of California* (after a trip to the West Coast) or *The ABC Book of the Smithsonian Museum* becomes a great learning tool and a memento of the trip.

Authors Emerging

Once children start writing books, they think of their own ideas. With a little help from her mom, six-year-old Madison made *I Like . . .* books about her favorite foods. These were simple little books made of folded typing paper, between four to eight pages stapled, with a colorful cover. She also made an *I Don't Like It When . . .* book (a good way to vent some negative feelings). The next year she went on to make a book on insects, which consisted of a picture and brief description of each insect. Whatever she was studying and learning about in her schoolwork, she often wanted to make a little book about.

Now Madison is in the fifth grade and writes stories and books on the computer. She has more ideas than she has time to write them all down. Karen, another child, wrote little books at home as a child, wrote a whole novel when she was in eighth grade, and has ideas for ten more books. The sky's the limit when we give our children the chance to be authors.

Making Your Own Supply of Blank Books

To encourage authorship, keep on hand some blank books so that when an idea hits for a story, your child has the available materials to put it in written form. A blank book can be as simple as three pieces of blank white paper folded, stapled along the crease, and covered by a construction paper cover that has been laminated (or covered with contact paper) after the title and illustration are done. This makes a pretty sturdy little book.

You can also make a blank book with a cloth cover. This method was developed by Posy Lough of the Posy Collection in Simsbury, Connecticut, who is not only a bookmaking expert but a crafts expert as well.

ASSEMBLE THE SUPPLIES NEEDED

Small Book	Large Book
1 piece of cloth, 10.5" x 15"	1 piece of cloth, 13.5" x 17"
2 pieces of construction paper in color to match cloth	2 pieces construction paper 8.5" x 11.5" in color to match cloth
2 pieces of cardboard 4.75" x 6.25"	2 pieces of cardboard 6.5;" x 9.5"
Small bottle of Elmer's glue	Small bottle of Elmer's glue
Needle with large eye	Needle with large eye
White thread	White thread
8 sheets of paper, 5.5" x 8.5" (standard white typing paper cut in half)	8 sheets of paper, 8.5" x 11"

PREPARE THE BOOK COVER

- Place the fabric on a table, right side down.

- Spread a thin coat of glue on one side of each of the pieces of cardboard. Place them glue side down on the fabric as shown, with about a finger's width (½") separating them in the middle.

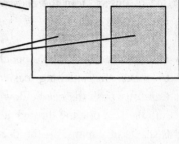

- Fold the fabric over the top and the bottom as if you were wrapping a present, and glue in place.

- Fold each corner inward to form a triangle. Then fold in the left and right sides of the fabric over the cardboard and glue in place.

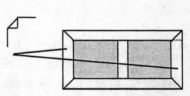

- Place a heavy object, such as a large book or dictionary, on the cover and cardboard and allow to dry.

PREPARE THE BOOK PAGES

- Fold the 8 sheets of paper to form the 32-page signature.

- Open the signature to the center. Mark two dots along the center line, each about ½" from the edge of the paper.

- Mark additional dots evenly spaced in between, approximately 1" apart.

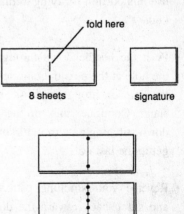

fold here

8 sheets   signature

• Thread the needle with about 36" of thread. Join the ends of the thread together.

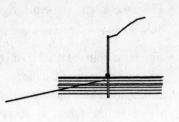

• Use the needle as a hole punch to make the stitching easier. Carefully push the needle down into the first dot and through all 8 sheets of paper. Pull the needle back out and continue to the next dot. When all the dots have holes punched through all 8 sheets of paper, you are ready for stitching.

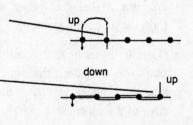

• Now, working from the back of the signature (bottom of the stack of sheets), push the needle up through the hole at the first dot. Pull the thread until about 3" remains hanging from the back of the signature. You will use this portion for tying a final knot.

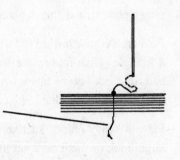

• Push the needle down through the hole at the next dot and pull the thread through until it is snug. Continue this up-then-down stitching pattern until you get to the last dot.

up

down

up

• Reverse your stitching pattern and stitch back toward the dot where you started, going down through the holes where you went up earlier and coming up through the holes where you went down earlier. Stop stitching when you go down through the next to last dot.

- Tie several overhand knots using the thread from the needle and the 3" of thread hanging from the first dot. Trim the thread close to the knot.

- Apply a piece of tape over the stitching along the spine (back) of your signature to stabilize it.

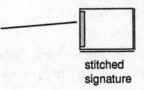

stitched
signature

FINISH THE BINDING

- Place a thin line of glue on the fabric between the pieces of cardboard.

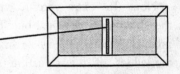

- Place the back of the signature in the glue and then lay it over to the right.

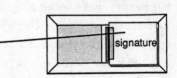

signature

- Spread a thin coat of glue on the surface of page 1 of the signature. Place the right end of the construction paper on it to fit exactly, and press down firmly.

glued
portion

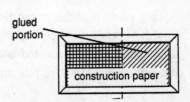

construction paper

- At the spine of the signature, fold the construction paper. (The fold will not be at the halfway point on the construction paper.)

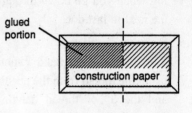

- Spread a thin coat of glue on the back surface of the left side of the construction paper. Press down firmly.

- Flip the signature over to the left and repeat this process for the right side of the book.

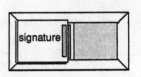

- Carefully close the book. Place a heavy object on the book and allow to dry.

Note: Be extra careful with the glue during the final binding process. Keep glue away from the edges of the signature so pages do not become glued together by accident. Use glue sparingly so that it does not saturate the paper or run out beyond the edges.

Your choices of fabric can make each book unique. Show your child how to do the bookmaking process and together make up a whole shelf of cloth-covered books suitable and ready for writing and publishing stories, poems, and journals.

Exercises

1. Have your child pick a favorite subject or hobby and create an ABC book on it.

2. After your child has created a book, celebrate by displaying it or having her read it to the family.

3. When you are reading a book to your child this week, point out the About the Author, the back cover copy, illustrations, and who the book is dedicated to.

CHAPTER 13

Writing Family History Stories

*Family storytelling lets
children in on the
magical secret that their
parents were once kids too!*
—Cheri Fuller

Do your kids love to hear stories about your childhood? Maybe they'd like to tell one of their own and record it for the next generation. Children from first grade up can write a lively tale about their family. It may be the most valuable story they ever put on paper. Written in their own words and style, the story chronicling their family's past can help them discover the richness of their family's heritage, bridge the gap between them and the older generation, and bring a strong sense of belonging and roots that many kids lack in our supermobile society.

Someone once said, "A person without a story is a person with amnesia." Many kids today have amnesia because they've never heard the stories of their grandparents and parents, much less seen them written down.

In contrast, when I've given young writers a chance to interview grandparents or relatives, the results are fascinating. Not only are the stories lively and interesting, but the kids themselves love the project. Here's one example in which a young fifth grade girl discovered how industrious and determined her grandfather really was in her rendition of "A Cow Goes to College":

Around 1932, my grandpa Maurice Howard graduated from high school in Tuttle, Oklahoma. He was eighteen years old and still wanted to learn more. So he decided he wanted to go to college. Little did he know that he was going to take a cow to pay for his tuition.

Maurice told his parents about wanting to go to college and they liked that idea, but it was during the Depression so they didn't have enough money for him to attend college. So usually people did not go to college. But Maurice was still determined to go.

He thought and thought and finally figured out a way: he would take a cow and sell its milk to make money for college. So Maurice took his cow to his professor. Maurice's professor agreed to accept milk in exchange for room and board. His professor even let Maurice take care of the cow in his backyard. And when Maurice was finished with college, he took his cow and went back home to work.

—Tammy, age 10

Ten-year-old Kelly wrote about her grandmother the gunslinger in her story, "The Guns."

When my dad was little, he and his brother would take BB guns and try to hit the head of a matchstick. They tried and tried but couldn't even hit the match.

A little while later, my dad's mom came out and said, "I can't believe you two can't even hit the match!"

My dad and his brother asked *her* to hit it. So she took the gun and shot the top "clean off" of the match on the first try! My dad said that she just got lucky, so she picked up the gun and knocked the match's head off again.

Soon they found out that when she was a little girl she could hit almost anything with a BB gun. They decided never to challenge her to shooting something again!

The young historians wrote amazing true tales: a dad who was stung by hundreds of bees; a grandpa who skipped church to ride horses and got bucked off, injuring his leg; a mischievous prank that turned into a kerosene explosion, grandparents' courting stories. The shared stories amazed their classmates, taught valuable lessons, and imparted a piece of history. For the writers, the stories helped them learn about their families. Relatives they never knew came alive as they interviewed and wrote family stories. By learning and retelling these stories, the children developed a sense of pride in their heritage and felt stronger ties to their pasts.

Digging Roots

To help your child write a family story, suggest that she learn about her family heritage by talking with relatives, especially the older family members, either by phone or in person. If your family has a geneological chart, show it to your child. You may want to share your own childhood experiences, happy and sad, with your child. If there's a family reunion or holiday gathering coming up, it's an ideal place to tape record recollections and ask questions.

By writing down the stories he hears, your child will learn many valuable language and writing skills. He'll also learn something very special about himself and his family. Before the event or before interviewing an older person, consider checking out some of the wonderful books for children at the library that can inspire their own family history writing:

Sarah, Plain and Tall by Patricia Machachlan
Little House on the Prairie, first in the Laura Ingalls Wilder series
Addie Across the Prairie by Laurie Lowlor
Grandpa—and Me by Stephanie S. Tolan
They Were Strong and Good by Robert Lawson

Path to the Past: Asking Questions

Good questions are the key to unlocking family history, and here are some that your child can ask a relative that will trigger memories and stir up stories. Have him pick five or six to ask during the first sitting:

- When and where were you born?
- Who were the first family members to settle in America? Why did they come here and where did they settle? Do you know any stories they passed down that show what life was like for them?
- Can you tell me what life was like when you were a child and during your growing up years?
- What are some of your early memories? Did you have any adventures that you remember? Tell me about your happy and sad times.
- What was school like for you? Did you have a favorite subject or teacher? Did you ever get in trouble at school?
- What were your favorite games, pets, or pastimes?
- Who were your closest friends and what activities did you do together?
- What was your most frightening time in childhood? Most embarrassing?
- What values and beliefs did your parents try to teach you to live by?
- Who influenced or shaped your life or career the most when you were growing up?
- What were your teenage years like?
- What was your first real job?
- How did you meet your spouse? What was courtship and marriage like? The birth of your first child?
- Did you go to war? Do you have any war experiences to tell me about?
- What have been the biggest problems, mistakes, or adversities in your life? How did you overcome them and what did you learn from them?
- If you could do anything differently in your life, what would it be?

Learning to interview a person is one of the basic tools a writer uses to get information. Developing these skills will help the young writer in many writing projects, as well as improve his interpersonal communication skills. Remind your child that listening is just as important as asking questions. The person's answers may prompt other questions and may lead to a fascinating story you didn't even ask for.

Looking at old photo albums is another good way to prime the story pump. Let your child bring along an album or group of family photos when he asks Grandpa about his experiences in school, in the army, or at another stage of life. Or get out some memory triggers such as a uniform, award, an old family heirloom or an object with meaning for the person. Maybe the person kept a diary.

Here's another effective tactic the young interviewer can use. Have him say to the person being interviewed, "Remember a specific age— eight or twenty years old, for instance. Share about the time during that period when you were the happiest, saddest, or the most frightened. Relate the dialogue between you and whoever you were with. Tell me the sights, smells, tastes, sounds, and feelings of the experience."

He could also ask the person to make a rough sketch of the house he was living in at that age to help jog the memory bank. These prompts help the person tap into memories he might not otherwise recall, and will provide the child with a wealth of information that he can turn into a wonderful story.

Give your child a cassette recorder and blank cassette tapes to use during the recording of the family history stories. He can also have a notebook and pencil to jot down details if desired.

Writing the Family History Story

Once the stories are gathered, it's time to write. Here are some tips on writing up the interview.

• Stitch together pieces of the conversation into one continuous narrative in the words of the interview subject. My children and I took this approach when we interviewed their Great, Great Uncle Silver Fuller at a family gathering one year. We asked him questions to jog his imagination and then divided his stories up, gave them titles like "John Matthias Goes to Dodge City," "John Matthias Meets Bat Masterson," "The Kansas Flood," "Grandma Fuller and Her Knitting Needles," etc. We did a little editing so the narrative would flow and Uncle Silver's voice would come through, yet we aimed to not distort the facts.

• Whenever possible, include physical attributes of people you're writing about, like facial structure, height, hair color, complexion, etc.

• Include enough concrete detail in your story so the reader can picture the scene.

• Use dialogue of people speaking whenever it fits.

• Put scenes and stories in chronological order, and include time transitions to help the readers follow your story or bridge to another one.

• Include a family tree—sketch a tree with all the branches of family members that you've discovered, or make a time line of important events and historical dates that affected family members. There are a number of computer software programs that make it easy to create a family tree by just typing in the names and birthdates of relatives; the computer prints out a professional-looking geneological chart.

• A poem could be written from the oral history or the results of the interview. Most any kind of writing can be a good format for family history and the rich imagery of poetry can be just right for preserving memories as the young writer's poem below shows.

Grandpa
His hair so short,
It's there, yet it's gone,
Reminds me of soft snowflakes,
That fall like dust to brush my eyelashes.
His eyes of wisdom,

Are filled with knowledge,
And the spark of a fulfilled life.
His skin,
Like a baby's wrinkled hand,
Dimpled with a sweet innocence.
His color tone reminds me of
Giant wheat fields whistling in the breeze.
His essence echoes of a loving care,
And I cherish every moment that I'm in
His presence.

—Cara, age 9

The family history stories can be typewritten and the pages photocopied and bound in loose-leaf notebooks so they can be added to. They can be handwritten in blank books that you create (see chapter 12 for how to make books for your child). Your child can include photos (copied inexpensively at the local copy or print shop so the old treasured photos don't get lost) and his own illustrations. When the book is finished, share it with family the next time there is a gathering. Digging up family stories and writing them down can be a great learning experience, a worthwhile task for any young writer.

Exercises

1. Tell your child a story from your own memory, or tell a family story that was told to you.

2. Ask relatives for favorite old family recipes and a memory or a little story to accompany each recipe. You might cook up a little heritage history.

3. If the grandparent or older relative your child wants to interview lives out of town or state, dialogue by letter (or E-mail) by asking one question at a time like "What is your first memory?" or sending along a blank cassette tape and a few questions for the relative to answer on tape and return. Then when your child gets the cassette tape back, he can write down the stories.

4. If older relatives aren't available, suggest your child sit down with senior citizens in your community and ask for stories about the old days, especially what life was like when the senior was the young writer's age or what he was doing at important times in history—Pearl Harbor Day, President Kennedy's assassination, or when NASA astronauts first stepped on the moon.

CHAPTER 14

Fun with Words: Word Play for Every Age

*The difference between the right word
and the almost right word is the difference
between lightning and the lightning bug.*
—Mark Twain

Just as the artist's paintbrush and paints are her tools, words are the stock-in-trade for writers. The larger the storehouse of tools or words, the more facility and power a writer can have. So playing games with words is like daily practice mixing colors on a palette, practicing a musical instrument, or stretching the muscles for gymnastics or another sport. Word play develops word awareness, stretches the vocabulary so the writer can pick out the best words and put them together to get his meaning across, and prepares writers for writing both poetry and prose.

The Wonder of Words

I remember the little rhyme we said as children: "Sticks and stones may break my bones, but words can never hurt me." Of course, the opposite was true. Early on, we learn that words pack a power of their own. Cruel words from a peer or sibling could cut to the bone, and encouraging words could warm the heart. Words are also full of wonder. Some words make us laugh and some pique our curiosity.

Words in a sad song can unleash a flow of tears and the lyrics of a patriotic song can fill our hearts with courage. From our earliest days we hear words—hundreds of them each day. Understanding those words, learning to use the right ones to express ourselves, and discovering new words is a process that continues throughout childhood, adolescence, and adulthood. The more words in our word banks, the greater our skills in speaking and writing. Children find pleasure in words that sound like their meaning—buzz, fizz, twinkle, and howl—and words that have rhyme and rhythm, from "Pat-a-Cake" to jump roping games.

Word Play

Here are some games and ways to play with words that increase vocabulary and language skill. You can engage in word play at home, at the breakfast table, while washing the car, or while driving carpool to stretch your child's vocabulary, boost reading comprehension, and improve writing techniques—all very painlessly and in an enjoyable fashion:

RHYME TIME

As you're riding along in the car, say a word and then have everybody name all the words that they can think of that rhyme with it. For example, *Clean:* bean, lean, mean, ream, teen, team. *Cat:* fat, sat, bat, mat, that, gnat.

HOW CAN YOU USE A TOOTHPICK?

This is a good brainstorming game that gets ideas and creativity going. Ask: How can you use a styrofoam tray, cotton ball, popsicle stick, fork, toothpick, computer chip, safety pin, T-shirt, or other object. Then name all the practical, crazy, or zany ways to use the object besides the normal use.

MAKE A WORD BANK

With a little index card file box and a stack of index cards, suggest that your child start building her own treasure trove of words to use in her writing. When she finds a new word in her reading, in conversations with people, in television programs, the newspaper, magazines, or advertisements, have her write the word on a card. She should then look the word up in the dictionary and write the definition on the back of the card. Encourage her to use the new words of the week in writing and speaking.

PLAY THE MYSTERY WORD GAME

This is such a fun game that one of the big game manufacturers brought out a commercial version called Balderdash, but you don't have to have it to play. The mystery word game painlessly builds vocabulary while stirring up kids' interest in the dictionary and learning new words.

You can play the game as individuals or teams. Each person has a little pad of paper and a pencil, and one person is chosen as the leader. The leader chooses a word from the dictionary (an obscure one is the most fun) and shows it to both teams. He or she then reads off four interesting definitions; one is the real definition of the word and the other three definitions sound like they might be, but aren't. The leader can make up the fake definitions or can peruse the dictionary and use definitions of other words.

Players select the definition they think is the correct one and write it down, passing their choice to the leader. The leader then identifies the correct definition, and players get one point for a correct definition. After a round or two, let players take turns being leader and choosing the mystery word.

WHAT AM I?

Did you ever play with riddles as a kid? "What's black and white and read all over?" was the first What Am I? I remember. My five siblings and I played this guessing game in the car sometimes for an hour or more on a trip. My children were equally entertained on a long haul by playing What Am I? "I've got eighteen wheels; I'm red and very shiny; I carry stuff . . ." Justin would say, and his brother would yell, "You're that Peterbilt semi that just passed us!"

Playing the What Am I? game is good for your child's language skills, and you can use the concept to produce some interesting writing, too. Suggest he write a descriptive paragraph about an object but not divulge what or who it is about until close to the end of the paragraph.

Here's such a paragraph. Notice how the writer doesn't actually say the name of the object he is describing until almost the last sentence.

Friend on My Left Hand

Way out in left field during my Little League days, he was my only companion. He kept me company while I waited on the third out and my pilgrimage back to the dugout. Studying grass, I let my mind wander as I chewed on the tough, salty string of hide binding him together. I used him to rub my sweaty, itchy nose, and I smelled the rich, brown leather which had become soft and perfectly worn. I spit on him and rubbed his malleable leather, just like the Big League players did. Impatient, I delivered occasional punches to my companion; I liked the pop of fist on leather. I offered a chatter of encouragement to my teammate on the mound, then I redirected my attention to my glove. Out of nowhere came the unmistakable PING! of bat on ball echoing through the park. The ball sailed in my direction. I extended my arm and felt the glove close snugly around the ball. You're out!

Writing Limericks

A limerick is a humorous, rhyming, five-line poem that children enjoy hearing as much as they enjoy writing. The rhyme scheme is a-a-b-b-a, meaning the first two lines rhyme, the third and fourth lines rhyme, and the last line rhymes with the first two lines. Limericks are often just one stanza long, and tell a simple story, but the narrative can be longer as this tale, "The Fate of a Rat," shows:

There once was a stupid old rat
Who also was very, very fat!
He lived in a hole
Along with a mole
And what do you think about that!

One day the mole and the rat
Went out for a friendly chat.
While having their tea
The rat said, "Oh me!
I fear we'll be lunch for the cat!"

As they raced back toward the hole,
"The cat is coming!" screamed the mole.
Oh me, oh my,
They had to fly
But the cat covered them with a bowl.

Oh no! Oh what would they do
They would call for their sister Sue.
But Sue was not there
And the cat couldn't bear
Not having some nice hot rat stew.

—Emily, age 10

How do you write a limerick? This humorous verse is built on two rhyming sounds, the rhyme of lines one, two, and five, and the rhyme of lines two and three. Clap out the rhythm together so the writer can get the beat, and then he'll feel the rhythmic pattern and be able to duplicate it. Try to have the first, second, and fifth lines containing no more than nine syllables each; the third and fourth lines no more than six syllables. Limericks often start with "There once was . . ." like this one does:

Hockey Cat

There once was a hockey cat named Fritz
Who ran a spectacular blitz.
He slipped on the ice,
Got up, said, "That's nice,"
Walked over and got first aid kits.
                    —Marshall, age 10

Always read the lines aloud after writing them to keep the rhythm bouncing along, and feel free to use your imagination to make up funny names and situations for your limerick, like the following example. The main aim of the writer is to bring a chuckle or smile to the reader, sometimes by a humorous character or by a twist at the end.

Poor Frank

There once was an old guy named Frank
Who lived in an aquatic tank.
He watched fish swim by
That really caught his eye,
but poor Frank! They sure smelled quite rank!
                    —Derek, age 9

Vivid Verbs and Knockout Nouns

The very best stories use active, vivid verbs and concrete nouns that create word pictures without even the use of adjectives and adverbs. Vivid verbs and knockout nouns liven up stories and poems and are fun to brainstorm with.

Name a verb and then have your children or group of kids brainstorm to come up with as many synonyms (words that can substitute for the same concept and essentially mean the same thing but with slightly different angles) as they can.

Start with *walk* and you may come up with:

amble, tramp, skip, stroll, saunter, hike, patter, trudge, slither, strut, swagger, tiptoe, shuffle, stagger, and waddle.

Try to think of synonyms for the word *house:*

shack, bungalow, igloo, hut, cabin, cottage, chalet, hovel, tenement, digs, pad, chateau, shanty, apartment, and haunt.

You can play the game in teams or as individuals. See which team can get the most synonyms. A thesaurus is a good tool for finding synonyms. The more you brainstorm with vivid verbs and knockout nouns, the more vivid the writing gets.

Kids can also brainstorm on synonyms for adjectives like these:

Bright: shining, shiny, gleaming, brilliant, sparkling, shimmering, radiant, vivid, colorful, lustrous, luminous, incandescent, intelligent, quick-witted, and smart.

Brave: courageous, fearless, dauntless, intrepid, plucky, daring, heroic, valorous, audacious, bold, gallant, valiant, doughty, and plucky.

Making Metaphors and Similes

Metaphors and similes are figures of speech in which a comparison is made—they are the stuff of poetry and good prose because they paint word pictures in readers' minds. With a *simile,* the writer makes a comparison of two unlike things using *like* or *as:* The cloud is like a spider, creeping on the ceiling of the sky.

In a *metaphor,* the comparison is implied: The night is a big, black cat.

Since metaphors and similes are important tools for writers, have your child create them, sharing orally and writing them down for future use. Provide a word and have your child describe it by comparing it to dissimilar things. Here are a few words to start with:

An orange (is or is like . . .)
My dog
The beach

Little brothers
A flag
The rain

Creating metaphors and similes can lead to a poem, and it is ideal practice for a journal. Skill with metaphors and similes will produce more vivid, lively writing that appeals to the reader's imagination and five senses.

Sensible Synonyms

Together, child and parent or teacher and student, should make a list of adjectives and adverbs that are repeated often in the child's writings. Each week one of these words is selected. The word is written down along with synonyms (*Big:* enormous, gigantic, huge, massive). The following week, the young writer aims to use some of the synonyms on her word list in conversation and in her writing. This is a great vocabulary and comprehension builder for students.

Tongue Twisters: Playing with Sound Patterns

A technique often used in poetry, title-making, and writing in general is alliteration, which means the repetition of the same initial sound in words which are close together in a line of poetry or prose. *Baby Betty buys ballons* is an example of alliteration. An extreme form of this technique is the tongue twisters. *She sells seashells by the seashore* and *How much wood could a woodchuck chuck if a woodchuck could chuck wood?* The *S*'s on the seashells always caught me, and I'd always end up in giggles. Tongue twisters are fun to say and write, and they don't necessarily have to make a lot of sense: *See the ragged rugged round robin run round and round the rugged, ragged, round rabbit* or *A chapped chap chops chipped chop tops.*

When your child gets really proficient at tongue twisters, you might want to challenge her to use the alphabet to make up ABC tongue twisters. This is fun to do with a partner. Take each letter and create a tongue twister for it like Angela and Rebecca did:

A   All American alligators are angry.
B   Bobby bought a box of biscuits and a biscuit mixer.
C   Cages of canaries crush crunchy carrots.
D   Dramatic dragons drag and drool desperately.
E   Elegant elephants eat endlessly.
F   Fighting fireflies flash fire furiously.
G   Graceful green gorillas grind granola.
H   Hyper hungry hugging hogs help hide hamburgers in heated
     hollow holes.
I   I see icebergs and icy igloos.
J   Jolly Joe jeers jokes joyfully.
K   Kicking cats care about caring kangaroos.
L   Little ladies love lacey lavender lingerie.
M   Movie makers make movies marvelously.
N   Noodle nibblers never nibble noodles nicely.
And on through the rest of the alphabet, ending with
Z   Zipping zebras zoom zig-zags at the zoo.

Tongue-twisting alliteration can also be used to write a silly story like this one:

The Bad Battle

The beavers had a big battle against the boring bulldog barking at the bear behind the barbed fence. The bear was bored from being behind the barbed fence in the barnyard because there were no big bad Barbary apes barking because the barebacked bear had barbecue that he stole from the boring bulldog who was battling the beaver because he barked bitterly at the bear in the barnyard behind the barbed fence eating barbecue!

—Mark, age 11

Alliteration doesn't have to be as complicated as tongue twisters. Subtle alliteration is used in titles, songs, and poetry all the time. But making up tongue twisters is a fun way to help kids be more aware of the sounds of words, and the use of alliteration will make their writing richer.

Quotable Quotes

This is an activity for the middle-school-aged child and up. Using a collection of quotes from books, newspapers, magazines, or other resources, have the child make a list of five to ten quotable quotes by famous people, presidents, Olympic gold medalists, or philosophers that particularly strike her or have something meaningful to say. Have the child read each quote aloud and try to figure out why the words in each quote make it so memorable and effective. For example, "Better to have loved and lost than not to have loved at all" was written by Seneca well over a thousand years ago. What makes it last and be memorable? Is it the brevity, the wise thought? Winston Churchill's "We have nothing to fear but fear itself" inspired a whole nation during World War II. Why did these eight words have so much power?

Encourage your child to continue collecting and jotting down memorable or impressive quotes she finds while reading. Then ask her to write a few sentences after the quote about why she likes it or wants to save it. She may even try writing her own quotable quote.

Writing Commercial Jingles

Have a group of kids make up a rhymed jingle for a radio or television advertisement:

- A shampoo that makes hair grow on bald heads
- A new kind of high-tech video game
- A fat-free chip
- Any other product they dream up

Word Stretching

Have a brainstorming session where kids have to s-t-r-e-t-c-h for words, think fast, and replace tired or boring words with words that paint pictures and provoke sensory images. Give a sentence like this one: *Maggie plays.*

Then ask, "What does Maggie play? Where does she play, and how does she do it? Is she enthusiastic about her playing? And who is playing with her, if anyone?"

One by one, each player can add something to the sentence until it might read: *On a dark, shivering winter night, Maggie plays her violin with so much passion that it lights up the room, warming all who hear her.*

To make word stretching more fun, add a time limit (stretch two sentences in five minutes, for example) or do it with a partner. A parent and child can be a team against two siblings or friends.

Exercises

1. Check out a book of tongue twisters and have fun reading some aloud (or have your child read them to you as you're fixing dinner). Then try to write one together and suggest your child write his own.

2. Suggest your child make up a simile or metaphor for one of the words listed in this chapter.

3. Help your child build vocabulary as a word detective. Get out a bunch of magazines, scissors, and a glue stick. Have your early reader cut out words that begin with *A*. Then have her glue them on a piece of colored construction paper. Each time you do the exercise, use a different letter until you go through the whole alphabet. Then staple the pages together to form an *ABC book*. An older child could look for and cut out verbs (action words), interesting nouns (people, places, and things), and adjectives and adverbs (descriptive words).

CHAPTER 15

Poetry Writing:
The Magic of the Written Word

Where do poems come from?
How do poems grow?
Do you find them in the blue sky
or in your mind's eye?
From colors and feelings,
nature and dreams,
Poems emerge from life's surprises,
and our imaginings.

—Cheri Fuller

For centuries, writers have tried to define poetry. "Poetry is like talking on tiptoe," said George Meredith. "Poetry is what in a poem makes you laugh, cry, prickle, be silent, and your toenails twinkle," said Dylan Thomas. One of my favorite definitions is Percy Bysshe Shelley's "Poetry is crystallized thought." Whatever your definition of poetry, I find that children and poetry are a great mix. From earliest ages, children love rhythm and rhyme, songs and sounds—ingredients from which poems are made. Poetry writing just comes naturally to kids. They put words together imaginatively in their everyday speech. That's why poetry writing doesn't have to be a scary or serious task. The short length, rhyme, and images (or word pictures) of poetry really appeal to kids. At the same time, the frugal use of words and preciseness in language we aim for when writing poetry is excellent practice.

Some poems reveal the feelings and emotions of the author. They speak to the heart (how it makes the reader feel) as well as to the mind (what it is saying) whereas an essay speaks primarily to the mind. Some poems tell stories, and some are fanciful, written just for fun. Poems look different than stories because they are written in lines and stanzas (a group of lines). Some poems are so short they fit inside a greeting card; they can say a lot in a small space. Some poems are rhymed while others are in free verse; some poetry is in a specific form like haiku and sonnets, while others grow their own shapes. Poems are usually pleasing to the ear, and the arrangement of the words creates special sounds. Some poems can be set to music and become a song. Poems are sometimes written to celebrate special events, like birthdays, weddings, and the birth of a new baby.

Children can write poems when they are happy or sad or when they just have something to say. One day we received this little poem, hand printed by our daughter Alison, a six-year-old:

To My Family,
My hart is for you,
And I'm for you,
And you need me to.

I'm not like any other person.
I'm just me, just for you.

Now I know that you love me that's
not a lie and I love you.
But you don't wurry,
I'm here for you.

And I'm here to stay too!

Alison was expressing her love, loyalty, and her own uniqueness to us, and a poem seemed the best way to do it. When difficult things happen in life, poetry can be the best way to express the deep feelings that young people experience.

When the Murrah Federal Building in our community, Oklahoma City, was bombed on April 19, 1995, poems literally poured out of children of all ages and adults, both in our state and all over the

United States. By writing poems, children were able to convey some of their pain, their questions, thoughts, and feelings through the power of words. Here is a poem about this tragedy by a young writer.

Crisis

Walking down the street,
Realizing the crime,
Seeing the building again for the very first time.

People reach up to wipe tears away,
Everyone stares and everyone prays.

Desperately trying to find someone to blame,
Oklahoma City will never be the same.

Blown-out windows, glass on the street,
But Oklahomans' strong spirits are far from defeat.

—Beth

The experience doesn't have to be as drastic as a bombing or the loss of a loved one to produce a poem. Poems come from our hearts and everyday experiences provide perfect opportunities for writing them. How can we encourage our children to write poetry? Here are some good ways to start.

Write an Alphabet Poem

First have your child write an alphabet poem using her name. The first line begins with the first letter of her name, the next line the next letter and so forth, so the poem looks like this:

J-arod is cool
A-wesome
R-eally good soccer player
O-n the go
D-oes like school

L oves kittens
E njoys reading books
S imply a good student
L ikes school
I s sometimes messy
E agerly plays volleyball

Add the middle and last name and stretch the poem the whole length of the paper. Name poems make wonderful presents: write about the birthday girl or boy and give the name poem instead of a card.

Alphabet poems can be written about favorite pastimes, sports, about seasons, news events, and all kinds of things. One young writer tackled the entire animal kingdom and alphabet by having one line and one animal for each letter of the alphabet.

A lligators ate amazing ants.
B ears balance big books.
C ats chase courageous cows.
D ogs dig dead doggy bones.
E lephants eat enormous eggs . . .

Suggest your child try writing an alphabet poem about his favorite sport like this one entitled "Baseball":

B aseball players everywhere.
A ll star games are played in here.
L ong-ball homers are fun to watch.
L osing is not an option.
P rograms are on sale!
A roma of hot dogs and nachos in the air,
R oaming people all over the place.
K ids are always having fun.

—Drew

Or if your child's interest is science or space, he'll like this alphabet poem called "Sun":

S un helps the earth from getting too cold.
U niverse is enormous open space with more than a thousand
   galaxies.
N eptune is one of the outermost planets from the Sun.

—Danny

Autobiographical Poems

Young writers love to reveal a little of themselves and this poetry form is a fun way to do it. Although these poems are built on a pattern, each one is just as individual as its creator. Here's what the poem contains:

Line 1: Your first name
Line 2: Four adjectives that describe you
Line 3: Daughter or son of _____ (or sibling of _____)
Line 4: Lover of . . . (write three or four of your favorite things)
Line 5: Who feels . . . when . . .
Line 6: Who fears (three things you dread or fear)
Line 7: Who would like to see (two or three countries, places, or
   things you've always wanted to see)
Line 8: Your last name

Cara

Shy, private, creative, happy
Daughter of Victor and Jill
Lover of music, books and art
Who feels relaxed when reading
Who fears failure, homework, and bad days.
Who would like to see China, Hong Kong, and
peace.
Chen

Color Poems

Color poems are fun to write and illustrate; children love to create them and share them.

Turquoise is like the moon glowing on the ocean at night
Turquoise is the eyes of a tired cat
Turquoise is like the color of the dim morning sky.
—Dana, age 9

Pink Is . . .

Pink is a bow in your hair,
A very pretty dress you wear,
A coat you wear on a winter day,
Covers when on your bed you lay.

Pink is a fluffy color,
a lemonade stand,
Pink is a heart on Valentine's
A flower in my hand.

Color poems are perfect for beginning poets because children find them easy to write, and they are confidence-builders. First, get the book Hailstones and Halibut Bones, by Mary O'Neill, at the library or bookstore. It's a wonderful book full of rhymed color poems or Adventures in Color, as the subtitle says. Reading it also helps the writer think about some different colors other than just the primary ones and the pictures stimulate illustrating ideas.

Here are the easy steps to write a color poem:

- Have the child choose a color and write it in the center of a piece of paper.
- Encourage him to look around the room and find the color.
- Tell your child to think about places and things that are the same color.
- Together, brainstorm and cluster ideas. One idea will lead to another. Do it fast to keep ideas generating. Don't worry what comes out. The results may surprise you.
- Then have your child select his favorite images and metaphors; paint a picture of the color with words. The poem will almost write itself.

When I worked with one group of children, we wrote a group poem first so I could model the brainstorming and clustering process. Blue was our first color. I asked, "What do you think of that is blue?

What are your favorite blue things—both indoors and outdoors?" I wrote as one of the children said, "A baby's tear."

Then, after asking, "What does the baby's tear look like and sound like?" someone volunteered, "The silent drop of a baby's first tear." Other images followed:

- Cornflowers spread over the field
- A scatter of rain
- Blue is the water in a swimming pool
- The night sky, the ocean, the birds flying in the sky.

Ideas and images generated more descriptive words. After we selected the best lines from our cluster to use in the poem, I wrote out the final copy on large paper and the children illustrated all the things mentioned. Then they wrote their own color poems.

I love this simple, short color poem by Valerie, age eight:

Blue is the twinkle in my best friend's eyes
Blue is the sky on a hot summer's day
Blue is . . . the ocean flowing softly against the sandy shore.

Color poems can be rhymed or unrhymed, long or short. Because this type of poem is so easy to compose, children experience success writing them and sometimes, when they get started writing about a favorite color they can't stop:

White

White is clouds on a warm summer day
White is light of the sun's warm ray
White is a shirt bleached in and out
White is the color of a piglet's snout
White is milk in a glass so bright
White is laces tied so tight
White is paint over a wall

White is snow packed in a ball
White is teeth brushed in paste
White is colorless without any taste
White is chalk scratched on the street
White is socks on smelly feet
White is a dove flying in the sky
White is a plane soaring so high. . . .

—Jesse Chow

Writing Poems with the Five Senses

When I've led poetry-writing workshops with children, poems that describe sights, sounds, smells, feelings, and tastes are among their very favorite kinds of poems to create.

The best writing, whether fiction or nonfiction, makes use of adjectives, verbs, similes, and word pictures that appeal to the senses. Easy to write, the poems can be just as creative, complex, or simple as the author wants them to be. Five senses poems help kids be more aware of using sensory images and description when writing stories and reports. They are ideal for individual or family writing activities.

In five senses poetry, the writer describes something abstract or concrete (for example, a feeling like *fear* or *courage*, an object like a *basketball*, a season like *winter* or *summer*, or an idea or quality) by comparing it with words that stand for things that we can *see, touch, hear, smell,* and *taste.* Here's how to begin the poem:

Have the child choose an idea, emotion, object, person, or sport that strikes him as interesting or that he relates to. Words like *wonder, anger, fear, friendship, storm, soccer,* and *ballet,* work well. The child should write his word in the center of a piece of paper and draw a circle around it. Then ask the child, "What is friendship?" or "What is spring?" One of the beauties of this kind of poetry writing is that when the subject is based on a child's interest or something he relates closely to, he tends to overflow with ideas. Ask: "What are the sights, smells, tastes, and feelings, that you associate with this word?"

When we used *ocean* for our word, we talked about what the

ocean looks like: "A big wall of blue separating us from down under!" said one child.

What does it smell like? "Salt seashells along the shore," said another.

As we brainstormed, the tastes, the feelings ("Like cold water rushing over your feet in the sand"), sights, and smells tumbled out, one after another.

You can explain that details and concrete words and phrases make the most vivid images, although there's no right or wrong descriptions in these poems. This exercise is especially helpful in teaching children that the images or word pictures they like best are the most concrete ones—the ones that remind them of real people, things, or events. Moving from the abstract (loneliness) to the concrete (moving away, an empty mailbox, a homeless person) also helps children learn to be specific and fosters critical thinking.

Brainstorm and write the images, phrases, concrete sounds, sights, smells, feelings and tastes that make the meaning of the word come alive as shown in the example below:

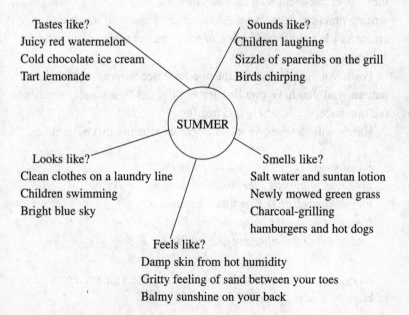

Tastes like?
Juicy red watermelon
Cold chocolate ice cream
Tart lemonade

Sounds like?
Children laughing
Sizzle of spareribs on the grill
Birds chirping

SUMMER

Looks like?
Clean clothes on a laundry line
Children swimming
Bright blue sky

Smells like?
Salt water and suntan lotion
Newly mowed green grass
Charcoal-grilling
hamburgers and hot dogs

Feels like?
Damp skin from hot humidity
Gritty feeling of sand between your toes
Balmy sunshine on your back

Have your child make a cluster with words and phrases radiating out from the core idea in the center. Using a circular diagram like the cluster will generate many more ideas than a linear (list) approach at this stage in the writing.

Share your cluster with someone, perhaps adding new ideas or expanding existing ones.

Begin to write the poem. Here is a sample poem written from the cluster above:

Summer Fun

*Summer sounds like children laughing as they jump in the
    swimming pool.*
Summer smells like chlorine water and suntan lotion.
Summer feels like the balmy sunshine warming our skin,
    tastes like ice-cold lemonade,
    and looks as hopeful and happy as the bright blue sky.

Once children have written one or two of these five senses poems, they can create them with ease and have fun while getting some good writing practice. Some young writers enjoy them so much that they create a little book or collection of ten or more poems celebrating the five senses.

For a younger child or someone who needs more structure and pattern, you can have one line for each of the five senses: touch or feeling, taste, sight, smell, and hearing.

Here's what a seven-year-old might write using this pattern:

Freedom is red, white, and blue like the flag
Freedom sounds like the birds chirping in the sky
Freedom smells like firecrackers smoking
It tastes like a wild watermelon
And freedom feels like my fuzzy teddy bear.

Suggest your child illustrate the poem and then mount it on a sheet of brightly colored paper to display.

Other good topics for five senses poems include: home, imagination, beauty, love, pain, jealousy, curiosity, happiness, war, peace; any sport like hockey, basketball, diving, etc.; snow, heaven, dreams; in fact, you can use any word that works.

Collage Poems

Collage poems are great for a rainy afternoon. Collect some magazines and newspapers, tape or a glue stick, and large sheets of paper (or butcher paper). Your child can look for words, phrases, and sentences that strike him or that are meaningful to him, catch his eye or ear, or cause him to laugh. He can cut out the words and phrases, arrange them in some kind of order, and then glue or tape them to the paper. The words can simply be a string of images and ideas, or they can follow a story line. The combination of words does not have to make a profound thought. The child might just like the sound of the words or the images may be pleasing to him. There's no right or wrong. The finished collage poem usually reveals a little something about what the child is thinking or feeling or what he's interested in at the moment.

See page 166 for an example of a collage poem.

Pattern and List Poems

Interesting poems can be created out of a pattern or first line that is repeated. Here are some starting lines for pattern poems and some sample verses:

- What if . . . ?
- If I were . . .
- If I were in charge of the world . . . (a take-off on Judith Viorst's children's book, *If I Were in Charge of the World*)
- I am a . . . or They call me . . .

Children are always thinking in what-if terms: What if people could fly? What if people had wheels instead of feet? What if we

INTEGRITY

Jessica

You ...

superior

special
values

OUTSTANDING

REPUTATION.

Honest

EXCELLENCE

TRADITION

Fortunate   Resilience   ENDURANCE

Collage Poem

could hear colors and see sound? They can turn their curiosity into poems. Here's one ten-year-old's attempt to do that:

What If?

What if the ground walked on people
instead of people walking on the ground?
Well, if the ground walked on people, we
would be smushed, smashed,
and as thin as paper.
We wouldn't be able to move a muscle for years, months, weeks,
*   days, hours, minutes, or seconds.*

—*Abby, age 10*

List poems are a form as old as "The Song of Solomon," the love poem in the Bible in which the bridegroom lists the beauties of his bride, or Elizabeth Barrett Browning's classic poem, "How Do I Love Thee? Let Me Count the Ways." The following is another kind of list poem:

If I Were . . .

If I were a car, I would be a big black Dodge Ram.
If I were food, I would be spicy hot pizza.
If I were a sport, I would be worldwide soccer.
If I were an animal, I'd be an American bald eagle soaring
*   through the air.*
If I were a building, I'd be the Empire State Building so I could
*   feel taller.*
If I were a planet, I'd be our own safe Earth.
If I were a movie, I'd be the best-selling movie, Jurassic Park.
If I were a pet, I would be a fish exploring the underworld.

—*Brian, age 11*

I Am

I am the firecracker that splashes in the sky
in beautiful color like dropping water on the ground.
I am a rushing waterfall running down into the river
like the rushing wind.
I am the basketball bouncing up and down
waiting for someone to throw me into the hoop.

—Kari, *age 9*

To encourage your child to write one of these poems, tell her to get inside an inanimate object, a season, something in nature such as a tree, river, or winter (as is written about below), a big league baseball bat, or a bed. Ask her to think about what it would be like to be that thing. This is a kind of personification (giving an animal or inanimate object human qualities such as thinking or feeling). Encourage your child to pretend to become an object or animal and then write as if she were that thing. What would she say? What is life like for her? What makes her happy and sad?

Here is one of my students' attempts to do this:

They Call Me Winter

They call me the winter
Everyone looks at my weak spots,
never my strong.
People say bad things about me like
"I wish winter never came."
But if I never came, there would be
No snow, not one
beautiful white snowflake.
Lots of bad things are spoken about me.
People don't realize if I, winter,
Never came there wouldn't be Christmas,
Snowball fights, or snowmen.

—Kim, *age 10*

Suggested inanimate objects or animals include a video game or computer, a dog, a lion, a clock, a running shoe, a tree, or a garbage can.

Cinquain and Haiku Poetry

Another type of pattern poetry is haiku and cinquain, in which the writer is given a syllable pattern to write with. The haiku, a Japanese poem, encourages conciseness (making every word count) and vivid imagery. Although writing haiku is sometimes thought to be easy, and the formula is simple, it's harder than it looks. I recommend it for more advanced young writers.

Haiku means *beginning phrase,* and it was originally the first verse of a longer Japanese poem. It consists of seventeen syllables, usually describing or symbolizing something in nature, the seasons, animals, insects, or flowers. Saying something in only seventeen syllables is a challenge. Here is the form, but keep in mind that modern haiku writers take more liberty in the number of syllables:

- Line 1: five syllables
- Line 2: seven syllables
- Line 3: five syllables

Read several haiku poems aloud with your child, counting the sounds so the rhythm and syllable pattern will be clear. If your child is interested in experimenting with the haiku form, encourage her to "take a photo" in her mind's eye of something in nature and try to write it as an image crystallized in time. Tell her to be just like an artist and try to paint a picture with just a few words.

A baby is born
in a hospital and cries;
his mother is there.
          —Jeremy, *age 9*

A cinquain is a five-line poem, and is easier to write than a haiku. Cinq is French for five. The tricky part is the syllable form:

- Line 1: two syllables, states the title
- Line 2: four syllables, describes the title
- Line 3: six syllables, expresses an action
- Line 4: eight syllables, expresses a feeling
- Line 5: two syllables, another word for the title

Short, five-line poems like this are good for beginners, especially if they write something from their experiences—a dream, a memory, or a vivid image.

The syllable pattern doesn't have to be rigidly adhered to, as the following samples show:

> *Music*
> *beautiful, slow*
> *wandering, drifting, relaxing*
> *puts me at ease*
> *sound*
> —Lindsey, *age 10*

> *Hummingbird*
> *colorful, musical*
> *gleaming, flying, sucking*
> *barely can be seen*
> *wonder*
> —Kelly, *age 10*

Hands That Tell Stories

Rough, callused hands; small hands with pale pink nails; hands with cuts and blisters—our hands tell stories and make wonderful subjects for poems. Children can write about their own hands or the hands of someone else. Here are some clues and suggestions to help the writer.

• First, look closely at your hand, perhaps tracing around it on a sheet of blank paper. Notice the lines, scratches, calluses, and nails.

• What stories lie in your hands? Could you write a poem about your hand using a simile or metaphor or description or a poem addressing your hand?

• If you are observing and writing about the hand of someone else, is the person's hand smooth or is it filled with many deep lines? What do these hands remind you of? What memories come to mind?

Here are some hand poems:

My Hand

I have a hand that is delicate
and light.
One scar to remind me never again
to fight with my brother.
My nails are shining so bright
like the school lights,
and too long to belong to me!
                                    —Brandy

The Hands I Will Always Remember

I will always remember my grandfather's hands . . .
The ones that had a lot of love and tenderness.
The hands that held me tight when I was little,
The ones that loved to play games with me,
hands that always comforted me,
The ones that never gave up,
the ones that now rest in peace.
I'll never forget my grandfather's hands,
the ones that I loved.
                                    —Katie, *age 9*

Poems as Presents

Beginning with the poems I wrote and tucked in their baby books, throughout our children's growing up years I wrote poems to them that I gave as gifts on birthdays, Christmas, and other occasions. On Valentine's Day, for instance, for our oldest son, Justin, I mounted this poem on a red heart with a white doily in the center.

A valentine for Justin
My blonde wunderkind
Who blesses us
With music, disguises,
    ideas bright
With noise, pictures,
    wild heady glee
Sometimes a dark cloud
    seems to shadow your brow
But oh, Justin, how special
    a son you are to me!
        —Mom, *February 14, 1977*

It isn't a great work of art, but it comes straight from the heart—and that's the best kind of gift. Poems like this have become a family tradition, to be created and given for anniversaries, graduations, and special times we've shared. My children all have reciprocated with poems of their own. I treasure all the original verses on greeting cards they made. I'll never forget the poem that appeared on my bed one evening with a homemade ring in a little box from our four-year-old, Chris. Early attempts were simple but filled with heart like this Mother's Day poem from Alison:

Mom—Your My favorite

Roses are Red
Violets are Blue
I hope you have fun
on Mother's Day
Because I LOVE you!!!

They also gave each other original poems as gifts. For Chris's high school graduation, Alison composed a seven-stanza poem entitled "Spread Your Wings," and carefully selected photographs of the two of them together at different ages, which she had matted and framed for him.

The heartfelt creations were and are so special. Just this week I spent time reading through some of their gifts. How priceless these writings are to me now that they are married, in college, and out on their own.

If giving poems as gifts sounds like an interesting idea for your family, here are some suggestions:

• Start small. Try composing a one- or two-stanza verse about how your child is growing or what she's like at this stage, and give it to her on her next birthday or special event.

• Start a new tradition of a Christmas blessing poem. Write a poem expressing what you appreciate most about each member of your family and stuff it into their Christmas stockings.

• Make a book of poems. When my friend Barbara's sons each graduated from high school, she created a special treasure in a leather-bound cover. Each page contained a poem written on a different subject—values and hopes she wanted to communicate and pass down to them.

• Try collaborative gifts. Louise and her son Aaron started a tradition years ago of creating an original Christmas card each year as one of their gifts to family and friends. First Aaron did the art and created the theme for the Christmas card, then Louise composed the poem to go along with his theme. Even when he married and moved away, they continued their collaboration by mail and made some wonderful memories with their joint project.

Exercises

1. Tape record directions on how to write one of the poems in this chapter. Let your child respond as per your directions. This is good practice in listening, following directions, and writing poetry.

2. Check out at the library and read aloud some favorite collections of poetry like:

> *A Child's Garden of Verses* by Robert Louis Stevenson (Platt & Munk)
> *Hailstones and Halibut Bones* by O'Neil (Doubleday)
> *Alligators All Around Us* by Maurice Sendak (Harper & Row)
> *The World of Christopher Robin* by A. A. Milne (Dutton)
> *Black Is Brown Is Tan* by A. Adoff (Harper & Row)
> *Where the Sidewalk Ends* by Shel Silverstein (Harper & Row)

3. Suggest your child write a color poem in her journal this week.

CHAPTER 16

Helping Young Writers Break into Print

*Publication of early work is what
a writer needs most of all in life.*
—*Erskine Caldwell*

Getting young writers' work published isn't the impossible dream. There are many magazines that regularly publish children's and teenagers' writing, and scores of writing contests where they can win computers, scholarships, cash prizes, and the best reward of all, they can see their writing in print. While there are many ways to publish or share children's writing, submitting it to magazines and newspapers is one way to challenge a young writer and find a broader audience. For a language-talented child or one who loves to write, submitting poems and stories for publication is not too different from an athletic kid entering a gymnastics competition, a musician performing for an audience, or a science whiz aiming for first prize in a science fair.

Child Authors Who Started Early

Many published authors got their start in childhood. Dorothy Clarke Wilson, a prolific writer of biographies of several U.S. Presidents and their wives and volumes of historical fiction, attributes her start in publishing to the fact that when she was ten years old, her mother helped her edit a poem and then encouraged her to send it out to a magazine. The poem was published, and her career as a writer was launched. She credits her parents' encouragement and support of her early work as a key to her development as a writer.

C. S. Lewis, author of *Chronicles of Narnia* and *Surprised by Joy* and many other books and essays, was only eight or nine years old when he started writing his first book, a fantasy novel called *Boxen*. Stephen King's first sale occurred when he was thirteen and wrote his first horror stories—his classmates at school bought the stories for a quarter each. Gordon Korman was in the seventh grade when his first Bruno and Boots book, *This Can't Be Happening at McDonald Hall*, was published. By the time he graduated from high school, he'd had four more novels published. James Cameron, who wrote and directed the movie, *The Abyss*, an underwater adventure, actually wrote it first as a short story when he was seventeen. What started out as a high school short story became a major motion picture. Bodie Thoene, once a Hollywood scriptwriter and now a best-selling historical fiction writer, got her start at age sixteen as a reporter for the local newspaper.

More recent child authors include Zach Robert and his coauthor, Mike Joyer, two eleven-year-olds who had their first book, *100 Excuses for Kids,* published in 1990 by Beyond Words Publishing Company. The boys compiled all the excuses they had heard their friends and classmates make for staying up late, not turning in their homework, or getting their allowance raised. They picked the name of a New York publisher out of the phone book, got their manuscript read, and had such successful sales on their first book, they wrote a sequel called *America's Excuses*.

Many of my students from creative writing workshops have had their work published. Nikki Buettner, a fourth grader, had her mystery story, "An Unexpected Guest," published in *Highlights* magazine. Emily Woodward, a fifth grader, received Honorable Mention and saw her personal experience story in print in *Byline* magazine, a national writing magazine. Others have had their writing published in *Clubhouse* magazine, school anthologies, college literary journals, regional newspapers, and other publications.

First Sale

My own children found publishing a doable challenge. Our son, Justin, at fourteen years old, wrote a poem for English class entitled "The Beach":

A young boy's anguished cry from a jellyfish sting rings out
While young girls giggle and rave over local beach lifeguards,
The roar of distant three-wheelers approaching—
these are the sounds of a summer beach day.
Later, darkness cools the hot sands
Waves lap softly against the shore
Only sea gulls cry
In the lonely stillness of the night.

His teacher added "Super!" to his grade of *A* for the poem, and he read the poem to the family at the dinner table. We enjoyed it immensely, and I asked him if he would like to send his poem out to a magazine for possible publication. "Why not?" he said.

We scanned a market guide that gave specifics on what magazines accept which kind of writing, and he decided on *Alive!* a magazine for teenagers published in Nashville, Tennessee. When their guidelines said most of the pieces in *Alive!* were short, and that they accepted poetry on their "Reflections" page, it seemed the right place to start.

Justin proofread his poem again, taking into consideration the editing marks his teacher made, and then typed it, including his name, address, and social security number on the page as they requested. To his surprise, a few weeks later, a letter of acceptance arrived with a check for $2.50. When the June issue of *Alive!* arrived in our mailbox, and his poem appeared with a wonderful illustration,

Justin was as excited as if he'd won the lottery (well, almost). This pretty cool teenage guy never spent the check from his first sale; instead, he saved it in a keepsake box.

Our daughter Alison's first published poem was a delightful piece called "Summer," which she wrote for her fourth grade language arts class. After receiving very positive feedback from school and even her big brothers, I encouraged her to send it to a children's magazine. Although she was paid in magazines instead of money (as many children's magazines do), the acceptance and publication of her poem in a real magazine was a high point in her year. Best of all, she kept writing poems and stories.

Children who see their work in print experience the sense of "I'm a writer." And having their byline in a magazine tends to motivate further writing.

Unfortunately, not all children are encouraged in their early attempts at publishing. Deborah Morris, the author of the Real Kids, Real Adventures series and other books for children, was eleven when she first decided she wanted to be a writer, but everybody told her that a writing career would be too hard. No one encouraged her to try to get her writing published. They said writers usually starved. They said she'd be better off with a real job. Those who discouraged her were wrong, says Deborah. "Writing is a whole lot more fun than most people think," she tells young writers on her Web site, Young Writers' Clubhouse. "If that's what you want to do, don't let anybody tell you it's impossible. Reach for the stars!"

How to Prepare Writing for Submission

Helping your child get his or her writing published isn't always as easy as our first attempts were, but it is very possible if you follow some basic guidelines and send the poem or story to a magazine that is looking for just that type of writing. Since there are over 150 magazines and contests looking for young writers' work, in addition to the growing number of on-line publishing resources on the Internet and World Wide Web, the opportunities are there.

For example, *Cricket League* magazine published in Peru, Illinois, has a contest every month for original poetry, stories, and essays by children. *REAL*, published in Kansas City, Missouri, has a page called "Art and Soul" for poems sent in by teens. *American Girl* asks for several submissions by young writers: "Speak from Your Heart," "Girls' Express," and answers to a monthly question like: "What simple pleasure makes you smile?"

Here are some publishing tips you can share with your young authors:

Revise, edit, and polish. When young writers submit their work to editors, besides having top-notch content, neatness matters, correct spelling matters, and good sentence structure and grammar does, too. That's why the child needs to revise, edit, and polish the writing, taking the time to proofread the final copy very carefully.

The final manuscript should be as free of misspellings and mechanical errors as possible, and it should be on clean, white paper. Although editors are aware of age limitations, they tend to favor writing that's neat, correct, and easy to read. You don't want a messily written story or poor grammar to detract from an original, creative piece of writing. So make sure your child prepares the manuscript with care before sending it out. A handwritten story or poem is usually acceptable from children if it is neatly printed, but if a computer or word processor is available, type the submission. Stories are double-spaced; poems are usually single-spaced. Each page should be numbered.

Here are some important things to look out for and make sure are correct before the poem or story is sent out for publication:

- Correct spelling
- Correct punctuation at the end of sentences: periods, exclamation marks, and question marks when needed
- Capitals at the beginning of sentences, proper nouns, and the first words in a quotation
- Correct use of quotation marks when someone is speaking
- Correct use of punctuation (commas and semicolons, etc.) within a sentence.

- Complete sentences
- Neatness and legibility

If you don't have access to a computer or typewriter, have your child neatly print the story or poem. You may want to print it for him if he has poor penmanship.

The author's name, address, phone number, and Social Security number should appear in the upper left-hand corner of the first page. A 1¼" margin on both sides of the paper and a 1" margin on the top and bottom is standard. Each page should also contain the writer's name and address in case the pages become separated. Most magazines that accept young writers' work also require that a parent or teacher sign at the bottom of the manuscript, saying that the writing is the students' own original work and that no help was given.

Decide the best place to submit the writing. Study the markets to find the right magazine for your child's work. Check the magazines you have at home, at school, and at the public library and write for their writer's guidelines, which will tell what they are looking for and how it must be submitted to their magazine. The writer's guidelines will tell things like how many words they accept (called *word count*) or what specific topics they need.

In the appendix you will find a list of magazines that publish children's and teenagers' writing, but for a more complete listing, consult *The Market Guide for Young Writers* by Kathy Henderson (published by Writer's Digest Books). It contains over 150 listings of magazines and contests looking for young writers' poems and stories, and their guidelines.

Write a cover letter. A brief cover letter gives the editor additional information he or she might need about the author and the writing. The cover letter should also let the editor know that the writer is familiar with the publication and that a SASE (self-addressed stamped envelope) is enclosed so that the author will get his writing back and notification of acceptance or rejection. If there is some unusual information the editor needs to know about the story or article, that can also be included. Here is a cover letter Darcy McCoy included with the story she submitted to a magazine.

> 1740 Morning Glory Road
> Edmond, Oklahoma 73013
> March 8, 1997

Student Page
BYLINE Magazine
P. O. Box 130596
Edmond, Oklahoma 73013

Dear Editor:

I am sending my short story to be entered in your personal experience story contest. It is a story about an experience that I had last summer.

I am eleven years old and I am in the fifth grade at Chisholm Elementary School in Edmond, Oklahoma. I write for my school newspaper. I like to sing, dance, and also enjoy art.

I hope you will enjoy my story and consider it for publication in your magazine. I have enclosed a self-addressed, stamped envelope.

> Sincerely,
>
> Darcy McCoy

Prepare two envelopes. One of the envelopes (called the SASE or self-addressed stamped envelope) is addressed to your child and contains enough postage to get the writing back after consideration. The other envelope is addressed to the magazine, preferably to a particular editor if her name is known. Darcy's envelope was addressed as shown on the next page. Although *Byline* is a nationally distributed magazine for writers, it just happened to be located in Darcy's hometown:

Darcy McCoy
1740 Morning Glory Road
Edmond, Oklahoma 73013

Student Page
BYLINE Magazine
P.O. Box 130596
Edmond, Oklahoma 73013

The self-addressed, stamped envelope is folded in thirds to fit into the envelope with the neatly folded manuscript. If there are a number of pages, it's better to use a 9" x 12" brown envelope instead of stuffing too much paper in a letter-sized envelope. Avoid folding artwork or photographs when they are being submitted along with a story. Last, be sure you send a photocopy of the art or writing you're submitting, never an original.

Next, play the waiting game. All writers have to develop a certain amount of patience because hearing from the editor can take up to six or eight weeks. (If your child hasn't gotten a reply by then, have him write the editor a postcard and inquire about the manuscript, telling her in a gracious way that if he doesn't hear from the magazine within a short time, he will send out the piece to another publication.) You may find your child beating a path to the mailbox every day to see if the acceptance or rejection is there.

If the piece comes back with an acceptance letter, celebrate with Oreo cookies and punch. If it's returned with a rejection letter, allow your child to feel sad for a few moments and then encourage him to get out the market guide and start looking for the next magazine he's going to send his writing to.

Having your writing returned is tough, but it happens to most writers. One of the world's top best-sellers, *Gone With the Wind*, was rejected over thirty times before a publisher saw its potential, so don't let your child get discouraged. Getting published is really about getting the right piece to the right magazine at the right time.

Before resubmitting, look over the work with your child and see if there are ways to improve it. When it is revised, polished, and ready to fly, send it out to another magazine.

Apply these inside tips on getting published:

• Seasonal material (like Christmas poems or Fourth of July stories) should be submitted four to six months ahead of the holiday so your child won't have to wait a year or more for publication. Magazines usually work months ahead, and the timing with which the manuscript arrives at their office can make a difference.

• Avoid sending the same story or poem to several magazines at the same time. If two magazines publish the story in the same month, it is a violation of copyright laws.

• Make sure everything submitted is your child's original work.

• Don't forget your SASE (self-addressed stamped envelope).

The Internet is a great resource for young writers looking to get published. Your child can visit Deborah Morris's Young Writers' Clubhouse at http://www.realkids.com/club.htm or http://www.realkids.com/. Young Writers' Clubhouse offers keys to getting published, tools of the trade, answers to frequently asked questions by young writers, on-line chat opportunities with real grown-up authors, and more. In addition, writing contests are held four times a year in which writers send in their work by E-mail and win prizes. It's a great encouragement for writers.

Inkspot's Resources for Young Writers is another great Web site that gives tips for aspiring young screenwriters, has on-line writing contests, and more. Through Inkspot's Resources for Young Writers, you can link to other sites for information on writing. The address is http://www.interlog.com/-ohi/dmo-pages/youngbk.html (direct Web page address or URL) or use http://www.interlog.com/-ohi/dmo-pages/writers.html.

While your child perseveres in her attempts to get published, always encourage her to continue to work on the craft of writing and improve her skills by reading as much as possible, writing regularly in her journal, writing letters, experimenting with different types of creative writing, and sharing her work with family and friends.

Entering Writing Contests

Another way for young writers to share their work is by entering contests. There are many contests for young writers, of all ages. Monthly contests are held by magazines like *Gifted Children Monthly, Byline Magazine,* or *Cricket Magazine.* There are also a variety of national contests and scores of local writing contests. There are essay-writing contests held by local Rotary, Kiwanis, and women's clubs and contests for special occasions like a Fourth of July patriotic essay held by local newspapers. There are also a growing number of on-line writing contests such as Deborah Morris's Young Writer's Clubhouse quarterly competition.

The prizes range from college scholarships—like the over $20,000 awarded to eight young writers in the *Guideposts'* youth writing contest—and computers, to plaques and certificates. Books, savings bonds, cash prizes, and issues of the magazine the piece appears in may be awarded, but the most important reward is the publication of the work and recognition in the magazine or newspaper.

When entering a contest, make sure you know all the guidelines and requirements for submitting your child's writing, especially the word count. It would be a shame to have a child's writing disqualified because the story is 1,000 words and the word count for contest entries is 700 words. Also note the deadline for entries. Make sure your child is in the right age group for the contest and that her work is appropriate for the contest. Finally be sure you sign the cover letter or entry verifying that the work is original and by the young author.

A Word of Caution

Parents, remember to not force your child to send off writing for publication or for a contest, especially if he is not interested or is hesitant or fearful of rejection. Submitting poems and stories for publication can be fun if the child takes some initiative after you make the suggestion. But there are many other ways to share without publishing in a professional magazine or winning a contest. Let's look at a few.

Create an Anthology

A worthwhile project is creating an anthology of young writers' poems, stories, and other writing. Collect writing from your child and his friends. This a great project for the next time they complain that they're bored and there's nothing to do.

Compiling an anthology of the neighborhood children's writing is a great way to encourage writing. It's a fun group project that can be shared with families and the community to celebrate literacy. Here's how to get started:

• Let everyone involved brainstorm to come up with ideas for a title and maybe a theme.

• Just as writers have editors that clean up their work before it's published, provide editors who confer with the young writers to polish their work before the final layout is done, so that spelling, punctuation, and grammar will be correct. Parent volunteers and/or older students can be helpful in this process.

• Let each person pick his two or three best or most favorite poems or stories to appear in the anthology, but at least one sample of writing by each writer who wants to be involved in the project is needed.

• If a number of different types of writing have been done, you can have different sections in the anthology: Personal Glimpses (for personal experience stories), Poetry, Family History Stories, Tall Tales, Mysteries, Limericks & Fun Stuff, etc.

• When the selection of pieces, editing, typing, and layout is complete, the anthologies are ready to be printed. Finding a local printer who will donate services or reduce the price (perhaps a parent of one of the writers) will help keep costs down.

• After printing, have an author's party, where the anthology can be signed by individual writers. Invite parents, teachers, siblings, and the local news media to the celebration of writing. Display the anthologies at the school library, local public library, and other places where people can read and enjoy the writing.

Churches can encourage their children to contribute pictures and writing for a Lenten or Christmas devotional book. When the Children's Council at our church embarked on such a project before Easter one year, they had a short writer's workshop to offer ideas and give the children time to write. They asked each child who wanted to contribute to write a short story, poem, or inspirational or devotional piece about Easter, or what they have experienced about God or about loving people in their everyday life. The children's candidness and creativity were a blessing to everyone who read the Lenten book and many adult lives were touched.

More Audiences for Young Writers

To share and publish poems and stories, writers can also:

• Have a reading club to read their work to each other.
• Read their writing to younger classes or groups of children.
• Write for the community newspaper. Encourage your local newspaper to have a "Kids' Column" or "Creative Kids" page so that

young writers can have a regular place to submit and share their best stories, poems, limericks, and art.

• Have your own writing contest. Make a brightly colored flyer and distribute it to publicize your contest. Decide on the type of writing you want submitted, the ages of participants, and other details, and ask local writers, parents, or teachers to judge.

Writing should be fun, and nothing is more satisfying to a young writer than sharing her work. Whether your child's work is published in a magazine or wins a contest, the greatest reward is praise from her parents. Your encouragement and support goes a long way in helping your child build a love for writing, gain confidence in her abilities, and develop strong writing skills.

Exercises

1. Get on a mailing list for the local bookstores so you will know when authors are appearing for book signings. The next time a children's author comes, take your child to the book signing and encourage her to talk to the author and ask questions.

2. Look at one of the magazines your child subscribes to or a youth magazine at the library. Find the page that is especially for children's work and for the next writing you assign, have your child respond to the question or contribute an idea or something that would fit the magazine.

3. Help your child start a writing and reading club. Provide a place for your child and his friends to meet, work, help each other edit, and share their work. Act as group leader if they ask for your help, or just serve cookies and lemonade and let them write on their own.

Appendix

A Grammar Guide

Standard written English has certain rules and conventions just as eating at a formal dinner party or nice restaurant calls for good manners. Learning the etiquette of writing is called *grammar*—the capitalization, punctuation, and usage rules that we follow when we write. Since the purpose of writing is to communicate to the reader, we observe these grammar rules to make our stories, reports, and poems readable and clear. And when it comes time for revision and editing, the more your child knows about proper grammar, the better she can improve both the content and the mechanics of her writing.

Let's look at some grammar skills that children learn at different levels in school. After you find your child's ability level, look on the following page at the punctuation and capitalization rules, parts of speech, and grammar problems you can tackle—step by step—as your child writes, revises, and edits.

GRAMMAR SKILLS FOR EACH GRADE LEVEL

Kindergarten:

Writes name using capitals and lower-case letters

Copies selected words from book or chart

Copies selected sentence beginning with capital letter and ending with period

First Grade:

Recognizes complete sentences

Writes complete sentences

Uses correct punctuation at the end of sentences

Capitalizes first word in a sentence, proper names, days of the week, and months of the year

Recognizes nouns

Second Grade:

Recognizes and writes complete sentences, including questions and exclamations

Uses correct punctuation at the ends of sentences

Capitalizes the first word in a sentence, days of the week, months of the year, special holidays, proper nouns such as names and places

Word usage: Is able to recognize abbreviations of months and days of the week, rhyming words, make contractions, use apostrophe *s* for possessives (boy's coat)

Recognizes antonyms (words that are opposite, like loud soft, cold hot)

Recognizes nouns, both common (general name of a person, place or thing—a president) and proper (specific name of person, place or thing—President Clinton)

Third Grade:

Writes in complete sentences

Recognizes nouns, both common nouns and proper nouns

Recognizes three parts of speech—subjects, verbs, and adjectives—in a sentence

Makes subject and verb in a sentence agree (*He goes*, not *he go*; i.e., a singular verb with a singular subject). See below for more examples

Capitalizes the first word of a sentence, the word *I*, and days and months

Capitalizes holidays, proper nouns, titles of books and songs

Punctuation: Uses quotation marks and end marks in direct quotations; uses commas in dates and after letter greeting and closing

Word usage and choice: Recognizes homonyms (there, their, they're; it's, its; know, no; ate, eight) and contractions

Recognizes synonyms (words that have the same or similar meaning) and antonyms (words of opposite meaning)

Fourth Grade:

Applies punctuation rules to writing sentences, including end marks, commas and question marks

Recognizes and writes different kinds of sentences: declarative, interrogative, and exclamatory

Recognizes and uses all eight parts of speech

Grammar usage: Makes subjects and verbs agree

Recognizes and corrects sentence fragments

Corrects run-on sentences

Punctuation: Uses end marks, commas and question marks; uses colons and underlining and periods with abbreviations

Capitalizes the beginning a new sentence, proper names.

Fifth Grade:

Uses correct sentence structure

Uses punctuation and capitalization rules in writing sentences

Recognizes all eight parts of speech

Recognizes synonyms, antonyms, homonyms

Word usage: Uses correct verb tense and makes verbs and subjects agree, uses specific nouns and verbs (word choice), uses modifiers

Avoids and corrects fragments and run-on sentences

Punctuation: Uses the semi-colon, apostrophe, colon, hyphen, and quotation marks correctly

Writes in compound and more complex sentences (in contrast to the simple sentences of the early grades

Sixth Grade:

Recognizes all eight parts of speech

Writes correct sentences (different kinds: declarative, interrogative, exclamatory, and imperative sentences)

Avoids and corrects fragments, run-on sentences, and comma splice errors

Applies punctuation and capitalization rules

Word usage: Uses difficult words correctly (can, may; lie, lay), makes subjects and verbs agree

Writes compound sentences

Corrects comma splice errors

Seventh Grade:

Recognizes and uses correct sentence structure

Applies all capitalization rules

Applies all punctuation rules

Knows eight parts of speech

Writes with modifiers

Writes in different verb tenses

Corrects misplaced and dangling modifiers; sentence fragments

Corrects split infinitive errors

Eighth and Ninth Grade:

Has mastery of capitalization rules

Has mastery of punctuation rules

Knows and uses eight parts of speech

Uses compound and complex sentences

Varies sentence structure

Usage and word choice

Has dictionary and thesarus skills

Uses grammar principles to expand and vary sentence patterns

Tenth through Twelfth Grades:

All of the above, including mastery and use of all capitalization and
   punctuation rules

Has the ability to recognize and use different sentence structures,
   eight parts of speech, and grammatical elements in sentences

Uses semi-colons, commas, and colons to create more complex
   sentences

Has dictionary and thesarus skills

Chooses the right word (diction) and is aware of word choice

Has the ability to avoid grammatical, punctuation and capitalization
   errors and to edit own work

USING CORRECT CAPITALIZATION

1. **Capitalize proper nouns**: words that name a specific person, place, thing, or idea. *The United States, Jessica Stewart, the
Danube River, Indian, Darden High School.* Capitalize the initials
or abbreviations that stand for those proper names. *C. S. Lewis,
J. D. Rockefeller*

2. **Capitalize proper adjectives:** a modifying word that is
formed from a proper noun. *an Oklahoma museum, Hawaiian luau*

3. **Capitalize the first word of every sentence, including the
first word of every quoted sentence.** *She said proudly, "I made
cheerleader!" The first hockey game is next Friday.*

4. **Capitalize the first word and every word except small
prepositions, conjunctions, and articles of titles of books, articles,
movies, and plays.** *Little Women,* (book) *Braveheart,* (movie), *"We
Are the World,"* (song) *"Phantom of the Opera"* (play), *Sports Illustrated for Kids* (magazine)

5. **Capitalize the names of religions, nationalities, lan-
guages.** *Australian* (nationality), *Spanish* (language), *Jewish, Chris-
tian* (religions)

6. **Capitalize brand names, official names, and organizations.** *General Motors* (name of business), *The American Red Cross*
(organization), *Post Sugar Crisp* (brand name of cereal). Note: Do

not capitalize the general word that follows brand name of product. *Colgate toothpaste*

7. **Days and months: Capitalize the names of days of the week, months of the year, holidays and special days.** *Thursday, Passover, Christmas, President's Day, January.* Note: Do not capitalize the seasons: *winter, spring, summer, fall*

8. **Always capitalize the word I.** *Last week I went to the library.*

9. **Capitalize the title of a person before a name.** *Judge Thomas Marshall, Senator Lewis*

10. **Capitalize geographical features such as bodies of water, islands, counties, states, cities, countries, continents, mountains, national and state parks, streets and highways** *Mississippi River, Alaska, Europe, Main Street*

USING PUNCTUATION MARKS CORRECTLY

1. **The period (.)**
   a. Used after a complete sentence: Mrs. Baker placed an order for a wedding cake.
   b. Used after an indirect question: The teacher asked when the school bus would be leaving for the zoo field trip.
   c. Used after a command: Please come here so we can read.
   d. Used after an initial, after abbreviations, and as a decimal. *(Susan B. Anthony, Ms. Jones, Ph.D. and M.D., 99.90 or $4.50)*

2. **The question mark (?)**
   Used when the sentence asks a question. *Have you ever flown in a hot-air balloon?*

3. **The exclamation point (!)**
   Used to express strong emotion, excitement, or urgency. It may be placed after a word, a phrase, or a whole sentence. *Happy Birthday, Sally! Call the police! Wow! That's a beautiful sunset!*

4. **Comma (,)**

   a. Used in compound sentences before the conjunction separating the independent clauses. *The swimming pool is behind the clubhouse, and the tennis courts are across the street.*

   b. Used to separate words in a series. *The American flag is red, white, and blue.* (Optional before *and*.) *I have a goldfish, a puppy, and a kitten.*

   c. Used after yes and no at the beginning of a sentence: *Yes, I want to go to the party.*

   d. Used after the greeting and closing of a friendly letter: *Dear Jamie, Yours truly,*

   e. Used to separate items in dates and addresses: *Our puppy was born on Wednesday, September 5, 1994. She lives at 123 Main Street, New York, N.Y.*

   f. Used after words used in direct address: *Josh, are you going to the basketball game? Are you feeling better, Aunt Corrie?*

5. **Quotation marks (" ") always appear in pairs.**

   a. Used at the beginning and end of a direct quotation. *Angela said, "That was a tasty, warm chocolate chip cookie." "I baked them myself," Sarah replied.*

   b. Used around quoted words when the quotation is interrupted. *"I am going," said Joel, "to the movies with my friends."*

   c. Used to set off humor, slang, colloquial expressions, or to draw attention to a special word. *We had a "blast" at the amusement park.*

   d. Used to punctuate titles of songs, poems, book chapters, short stories, magazine and newspaper articles. *"This Land Is Your Land"* (song) *"The Adventure of the Red Circle"* (short story) *"The Princess"* (poem) *"The Plight of the Homeless"* in <u>The New York Times.</u>

   e. Used to explain foreign words: *Adios means "goodbye" in Spanish.*

Hints on usage of quotation marks:

- When using other punctuation marks at the end of a quoted passage, always keep the punctuation *before* the end quotation mark. *Our choir sang, "This Land is Your Land."*
- To use a quotation within a quotation, The student said, "I think the line from *The Courtship of Miles Standish* was 'So the strong will prevailed, subduing and moulding the gentler, Friendship prevailed over love, and Alden went on his errand.' "
- A question mark or an exlamation point is placed *inside* the quotation marks when it punctuates the quotation; it is placed *outside* when it punctuates the main sentence. *She screamed, "Don't drop the ball!" Can you believe she recited "The Gettysburg Address"?*

Shortcut: If your child is having a difficult time distinguishing which words should go inside the quotation marks, draw a big open mouth and put "and" (quotation marks like dimples on the cheeks) on each side of the mouth. Say, "The only words that you put *inside* the quotation marks are the words that actually come out of the person's mouth." (Not the *he said* or *she exclaimed*.)

6. **The em dash (—)**
    a. Used with a parenthetical or explanatory remark within the sentence: *Tom Cruise—to say the least—is very good looking! She was a truly gracious woman—the best I ever met.*
    b. The dash is used to show a sudden break in the sentence. *The hockey stick—if you didn't notice—is damaged on the end.*
    c. The dash is used to show that a character's speech is interrupted by another person. *Right—yes, I would—I'd love to go to the opera!*

7. **Underlining (_____)**
    a. Used to indicate the title of a book or magazine. <u>The Washington Post</u>, <u>National Geographic</u>

b. Used to show emphasis in a sentence. Underlining empha-sizes a word that's very important.

8. The hyphen (=)

Used to divide or join words, and to create new words: *That intern position provides great on-the-job training.*
His plan was half-baked, so we decided not to follow it.
Peggy's self-esteem was at an all-time high after she won the diving championship.

9. The parenthesis ( )

a. Used as an optional form of punctuation (instead of commas and dashes) to set off parenthetical or nonessential words or phrases in a sentence. *Thomas Edison (a real genius) invented the light bulb and the record player.*
b. Used to enclose words that give additional information or make the meaning clearer. *The diagram (figure two) will help you understand how to put the bicycle together correctly.*

10. The apostrophe (')

a. Used to show possession. *The Senator's office is huge.*
b. Used to show omission of letters, as in a contraction. *We'd be happy to come to your party.* Also *can't, won't.*
c. Used in plural possessive: *The girls' volleyball team*

Shortcut: To choose between *it's* and *its*, substitute "it is" in the sentence:

The puppy bit (its or it's) tail. (Since "the puppy bit *it is* tail" wouldn't make sense, you choose *its*.)
(Its or It's) raining. (*It is raining* is the best choice so *its* is incorrect.)

11. The semi-colon (;)

a. Used to separate independent clauses. *Your mother called while you were out; she said to call her back.*

b. Used to separate phrases or clauses in a series when one contains a comma. *The tour included Bern, Switzerland; Paris, France; and Stuttgart, Germany.*

c. Used before however, thus, yet. *Janice did her gymnastics practice every day; however, she was not prepared for the stiff competition at the finals.*

d. Used before the conjunction in a long compound sentence containing a comma in the independent clause. *The musicians beat loudly on a strange collection of instruments including a hollowed log, a kind of tambourine, and elephant hide drum; and a young girl, after the noise began, got up to dance.*

Tips on semi-colon usage: The semi-colon is a cross between a period and a comma. It can sometimes be used in place of a period, and is a handy solution for run-together sentences.

12. The colon (:)

a. Used to indicate that a list will follow. *On our vacation we tried the following sports: scuba diving, hiking, and swimming.*

b. Sometimes used after a salutation of a business letter. *Dear Ms. Donnelly:*

c. Used between numbers in time. *The cross-country meet starts at 2:30 p.m.*

d. Used to introduce a formal quotation in an essay or report. *President Clinton said in his acceptance speech: "We will build a bridge to the 21st Century!"*

13. Ellipsis (...)

a. Used to show omitted words or sentences or to indicate a pause in dialogue. *That's the last thing I remember . . . and then I became unconscious. "That's . . . amazing!" Marianne cried.*

Tip: When typing an ellipsis, leave one space before, after, and between each period.

THE EIGHT PARTS OF SPEECH

The words in the English language have been classified into eight different groups called the *parts of speech*. Knowing the parts of speech is helpful—it gives us a vocabulary to talk about how words are used in sentences, to improve sentence structure, and to learn more about our language.

The Eight Parts of Speech Are:

1. **Nouns:** the name of a person, place, thing, or idea. Proper nouns are specific names of a person place or thing. (*Mary, Texas, Washington Monument*) Common nouns are general people, places or things. (*teacher, the park, book*)
2. **Pronouns:** words used in the place of nouns. (*I, you, he, she, we*) Possessive pronouns are *hers, his, ours*.
3. **Verbs:** words that show action or state of being. (*fly, run, are, feel*)
4. **Adjectives:** words that describe or modify nouns and pronouns. (*funny joke, short story, happy baby*).
5. **Adverbs:** words that modify or tell something more about a verb, adjective, or another verb. (*he took the turn smoothly, the candles glowed brightly*).
6. **Conjunctions:** connect words or groups of words. (*and, or*)
7. **Prepositions:** words that show how a noun is related to other words in the sentence. (*over, under, near*)
8. **Injections:** words that express emotion or surprise. (*Hey! Wow!*)

Shortcut: The major parts of a sentence are the *subject* (the name of the person, place, or thing) and the *verb*.

To find the subject in a sentence, find the action word (verb) and then ask *who* or *what* after the verb.

To find the active verb, ask: *What is the subject doing?*

Help your child figure out what the word is *doing* in the sentence and he'll be able to identify the part of speech. Ask: What is this word's job? Is it naming something? Is it describing something? Is it showing action? Is it joining words together?

You can teach your child these eight parts of speech by discussing each word and giving examples that he can relate to (for example: for a proper noun, his name, and for a common noun, an object in his room). Let your child cut out words and pictures of objects from magazines that represent the different parts of speech. Then when you are assisting in the editing process and correcting mechanical errors in writing, you can refer to the words by what part of speech it is. By understanding how our language works, we become better speakers and writers!

Note that certain of the parts of speech are best taught at certain ages and grade levels. For example, first graders should learn to recognize nouns. Second graders can identify common and proper nouns, whereas third graders can learn to recognize verbs, adjectives, and nouns as the subject of a sentence. This will help you teach the parts of speech at an appropriate time your child can both learn and apply to his writing.

COMMON GRAMMATICAL MISTAKES

Many writing problems can be taken care of if students learn how to correct and avoid grammatical errors. But first they need to know what those errors are. The following are the most common errors made in writing sentences that your child will need to learn in order to revise and edit her writing.

It is also helpful to have a grammar handbook on hand. The Recommended Reading section suggests several good ones. In addition, a dictionary and thesaurus are good tools for writing and revising. You could also get a notebook for your child to record frequently made grammatical mistakes.

Sample sentences are included with each grammar problem below.

1. Run-on sentences: When two sentences are joined without any punctuation mark or conjunction (and, but), then you have a run-on sentence. If the two sentences could stand on their own (i.e., are complete thoughts) then you need end punctuation (a period) or a connecting word and comma. Reading the sentence aloud always helps the discovery of a run-on error and helps you decide *where* to put the period, semi-colon, or connecting word and comma.

Put the proper punctuation in the run-on sentences below:

I thought the game wasn't fair we should have won!

I don't want to go to school I've not finished my homework I want to play instead.

2. Sentence fragments: To be correct, a sentence is supposed to have a subject and a verb. A sentence fragment is an incomplete sentence, or a group of words that *does not* express a complete thought. It leaves out some of the information, usually either the subject or the verb, that the reader needs to make sense of the sentence.

Correct the sentence fragments below:

Thinks she is so smart.

Because we wanted to stay all night at Sally's house.

Not fun to me.

3. Subject and verb agreement: The subject and verb need to agree in number. A singular verb is to be used when the subject in the sentence is singular, and a plural verb is needed for a plural subject. (Example: *Cucumbers taste like straw to me.* (The subject *cucumbers* and the verb *taste* are both plural)

Choose a verb to match or agree with the subject in the sentences below:

The girl _____ a cat in her bedroom. (has, have)

The girls _____ a cat in their bedroom. (has, have)

Students _____ happy when they make As on their report card. (is, are)

Justin _____ turkey and cheese sandwiches for lunch. (eat, eats)

4. Pronoun Agreement: Choose pronouns that agree with the words they replace in the sentence.

Choose the right pronouns in the sentences below:

If my sister and her two friends eat a large pizza, _____ will be so full they can't trampoline. (she, they)

John's skis look smooth now that _____ have been cleaned and sanded. (he, they)

Caroline practices piano whenever _____ can after school. (she, he)

Shortcut on Pronoun Agreement: Deciding when to use "me" and when to use "I" can be puzzling in a sentence like this one:

Is Mom going to take Jennifer and _____ to the park? To pick the pronoun that agrees, take out the receiver of the action, Jennifer, and ask *Is Mom going to take (I or me?) to the park?* Now try these two:

Would you give Brian and _____ some pizza?

Jill and _____ are going to the baseball game.

5. Misplaced or dangling modifiers: When a modifier (a describing word like an adjective or adverb) is in the wrong place in a sentence, it can change the entire meaning of the sentence and confuse the reader. For example:

Megan said that at six years old her mother wouldn't let her ride a bike. (Is Megan six years old or is her mother six years old? It's hard to tell.)

To correct, move the modifying phrase or words so that the meaning is clear:

When Megan was six years old her mother wouldn't let her ride a bike. Try to correct these sample exercises:

When sitting, my shoulders slump back in the chair.

He fell while he was running into a manhole.

The woman who was cooking quickly swallowed the artichokes.

6. Split infinitives: An infinitive is made up of *to* plus a verb. A split infinitive error is made when you wedge an adverb between "to" and the verb in a sentence like this: *I need to quickly eat my breakfast so I won't be late for school.*

The dog began to industriously dig in the backyard, looking for a hidden bone.

To correct the split infinitive, shift the adverb out of the wedge of the infinitive to a part of the sentence in which it would flow more smoothly:

I need to eat my breakfast quickly so I won't be late for school.

The dog began to dig industriously in the backyard, looking for a hidden bone. Correct these split infinitives:

I started to fast and furiously paddle upstream.

My cat began to hastily jump on the kitchen counter for a treat.

7. Comma splice: The comma splice error is made when you run two sentences together with only a comma between them instead of a period:

I don't want to go over to Carrie's house, I don't like her.

Actually these are two complete thoughts that could stand alone, so they need their own end punctuation. You can correct by putting a period after *house*, or you can use a semi-colon after *house*. You could also put a connecting word like *and* or *because* after house: *"I don't want to go over to Carrie's house, because I don't like her."*

A good example of a sentence in which you need a comma to correct the comma splice error is: *We packed all our luggage, then we were on our way to the airport. (We packed all our luggage, and then we were on our way to the airport.)*

Correct these sentences with comma splice errors:

Dallas is a big metropolitan city, thousands of cars, trucks, buses, and motorcycles move through it every day.

Maggie didn't make it to the party on time, therefore we had to go ahead with the dinner.

Guidelines for Assessing Children's Writing

Parents who teach their child at home have often told me they have much difficulty in knowing how to access their child's writing. They've asked questions like: "What is an *A* composition?" "How can I decide on criteria to evaluate her writing so it's just not based on how I feel on a certain day?"

While we don't want to put our whole focus on producing a finished product to grade, having guidelines to evaluate your child's writing will help you set standards of excellence and help your child aim for them.

Assessment or Evaluation of writing should:

- give children a sense of their progress
- motivate and facilitate their learning to write
- help them set goals about where they need to improve and what to aim for

Keep in mind:

- Everything children write doesn't need to be graded or assessed.
- If children are writing every day, you can pick out one or two assignments each week to evaluate.
- When you do evaluate writing, consider: **content** (what the story or report is saying) and **mechanics** (spelling, grammar); **The writing process** (the different stages and drafts your child went through to produce the piece of writing; how well she entered into pre-writing, drafting the story, revising and editing it), and **the finished product.**
- Inform children of the standards or criteria for each piece of writing and when possible, involve them in helping set the standards of what an *A, B, C*, etc., paper is.
- Your evaluation should help give a fairly accurate picture of current writing skills and what needs to be worked on in the next writing assignment.

Here are some tools that will help in evaluating writing:

1. **A checklist:** Clip to the individual writing assignment and keep it simple. Think through your goals for this particular piece of writing and connect the goals to the checklist. You can use the checklist to analyze your child's progress over a nine-week period or a

semester. When complete, add some written comments to the check-list about progress, confer with the child, and have him file it in the writing folder.

A Sample Checklist for a 6th grader:
- introduction is effective and grabs reader's attention
- ideas are in logical order
- good word choice
- things are arranged together in a paragraph that goes together
- good wrap-up (concluding sentence)
- correct punctuation
- correct spelling
- correct capitalization

A Sample Checklist for a 3rd grader:
- periods at the ends of sentences
- complete sentences
- readable handwriting
- compound sentences connected with conjuntions *and, but, or*
- correct capitalization

2. **Assign point values to parts of the writing process:** In order to demonstrate the importance of each stage of the writing process, you can assign a certain number of points to each of the five steps, to equal 100 points on any given assignment. For example:

20 pts. Prewriting—This can include any number of prewriting activities, depending on the assignment, such as inter-viewing, freewriting, mapping, etc.

20 pts. Drafting—Selects topic, completes first draft and moves through several drafts.

20 pts. Revising—Rearranges, adds, or deletes material to improve story, puts events in logical order, shows enthu-siasm for revising, improves word choice with vivid verbs, adjectives and adverbs.

20 pts. Editing—Reads paper aloud to edit, uses checklist to

proofread, checks grammar and punctuation, makes an effort to eliminate errors in spelling, uses resources like dictionary, thesarus, etc.

20 pts.   Publishing—Shares story orally with class, family, or others, uses a creative way to share the writing with a wider audience.

3. **Portfolio assessment:** The Portfolio is a writing folder that is turned in at the end of a grading period. The portfolio gives a picture of the writer's progress with a collection of writing samples—for example: a poem, a personal experience story, ten journal entries, a book report, or a creative writing sample. The portfolio may be evaluated for the nine-week period or the semester. Points are given for each piece of writing in the portfolio.

4. **Traditional grading:** Two grades for each writing assignment are given, one for content and one for mechanics—with criteria determined before writing.

For example, for one story-writing assignment:

CONTENT — Uses interesting lead, uses creative sentence starters, shows imagination, shows wide vocabulary or good word choice

MECHANICS — Uses periods correctly with no run-on sentences, uses capitals correctly, correct spelling

On the mechanics portion of the grade, pick the most important, age-appropriate skills that your child has been working on and base your evaluation on those skills.

For another assignment:

CONTENT — Good introduction and ending, uses at least four examples with supporting details, organizes ideas, writes with the five senses

MECHANICS — Varied sentence form and length, legible writing, consistent verb tense, correct punctuation, spelling and capitalization

The content and mechanics letter-grading tends to be more subjective and teacher-directed.

5. **A rubric** is a scoring guide that lists the criteria and tailors the criteria to a specific writing assignment or activity. It gives students a focus and a way to know just what's expected in the piece of writing. The student sees what to aim for and what is going to contribute to an *A* paper (clearly explained directions, detail, correct punctuation and spelling, for example). Since the rubric is somewhat complicated, it may work best for upper elementary to high school.

If it is used in the lower grades, the rubric needs to be simplified and shortened.

One advantage of the rubric is the student can use it for self-assessment before turning in the paper, or classmates can help score each other's papers. In any case, students like to know what's expected and a scoring guide, when well constructed, can help them know what mark they are trying to hit and enable them to see their strengths and weaknesses in the post-writing stage.

For example, for a paper on "How to Make a Peanut Butter Sandwich," here are the key elements for a paper assigned an:

A (or 5) Excellent Paper
- Engaging or creative introduction
- Directions clearly explained
- Directions in proper order for reader to actually follow
- Sufficient detail given
- Effective conclusion
- Composition written in paragraphs
- Correct punctuation and capitalization used
- Neatness and correct spelling

In contrast to the:

D (or 2) Needs Improvement Paper
- Directions difficult to follow
- Directions confusing
- Frequent sentences errors in usage, mechanics, or structure
- Handwriting difficult to read
- Frequent misspellings

Magazines That Publish Young Authors

If your child has written something with a fresh idea that is creative and original or with a humorous approach, consider letting him share it with other children. In doing so, you give your child a broader audience and encouragement to keep writing. Seeing their writing in print is exciting to most young writers.

Generally, submissions should be neatly printed or typed. Name, age, school, and full address should be included. Whether a poem, story, or drawing, be sure it is your child's very own, original work. If you want it returned, send a self-addressed stamped envelope. For more guidelines on preparing writing for submission, see chapter 16. Be sure to write for their writer's guidelines and monthly themes if you are interested in submitting work to a magazine.

Some of the many magazines that publish the writing of children include:

Boy's Life: 1325 West Walnut Hill Lane, P.O. Box 152079, Irving, TX 75015-2079. The "Reader's Page" accepts jokes and interesting hobby ideas, in addition to responses to questions like "Have you had an adventure lately?" Writers must be under eighteen years of age.

Children's Digest: P.O. Box 567, Indianapolis, IN 46206. This magazine accepts poetry, fiction, nonfiction, jokes, and riddles—all health-related—by eight- to thirteen-year-olds.

Children's Playmate: P.O. Box 547, Indianapolis, IN 46206. Children ages six to eight are encouraged to send original drawings, poems, jokes, and riddles.

Clubhouse, published by Focus on the Family, 8605 Explorer Drive, Colorado Springs, CO 80920. Children's responses to the editor's questions such as, "What is the funniest thing that ever happened to you?" or "What do you like most about Christmas?" are published monthly.

Cobblestone Magazine: 20 Grove Street, Peterborough, NH 03458. This is an American history magazine for children. Send letters, drawings, and short poems to "Dear Ebenezer." Ebenezer also asks questions each month, and *Cobblestone* publishes the children's answers in the next issue. Write for guidelines and monthly themes.

Creative Kids: The National Voice for Kids, P.O. Box 8813, Waco, TX 76714-8813. *Creative Kids* encourages children age eight to fourteen to send in their stories, games, puzzles, poetry, artwork, and photography. Writing must be sent with a self-addressed stamped envelope.

Cricket Magazine: Cricket League, P.O. Box 300, Peru, IL 61354. *Cricket* has a monthly poetry, story writing, and art contest for children age thirteen and younger. Write for details and contest themes.

Highlights for Children: Honesdale, PA 18431. This is a tough magazine to get published in because they get so many submissions, but I have had a few students whose writing was published on "Our Own Pages." They accept original poems, stories, and black-and-white drawings. The writer must include name, age, and home address, and the submissions are not returned.

Jack and Jill Magazine: 1100 Waterway Blvd., P.O. Box 547, Indianapolis, IN 76206. For seven- to ten-year-olds; send original drawings or poems with your name, age, school, and address.

practical homeschooling: Home Life, P.O. Box 1250, Fenton, MO 63026-1850. *Practical Homeschooling* offers monthly writing contests to paid subscribers with two age categories: ages nine and under, and ages ten and up. Winners' work is published in the magazine. Entries are not returned.

Penny Power, P.O. Box 54861, Boulder, CO 80322-4861. If you have something you'd like to share about managing or making money, successful science fair projects, or questions, send your letter to *Penny Power*. Reading the magazine and responding to the "Pen Power" page is your best bet with this magazine.

Skipping Stones, P.O. Box 3939, Eugene, OR 97403. Multicultural children's magazine that features writing and art by children age seven to eighteen and connects children from any country with a pen pal. Write for free guidelines and enclose a self-addressed stamped envelope.

Stone Soup: The Magazine By Young Writers and Artists. Children's Art Foundation, P.O. Box 83, Santa Cruz, CA 95063 (800) 447-4569, is a literary magazine containing stories, poems, book reviews, and art by children up to age thirteen. Published by the Children's Art Foundation, a nonprofit educational organization devoted to encouraging children's creativity. Send submissions of stories (any length), poems, art (pictures accepted in any size or color), and book reviews.

SOME MAGAZINES THAT PUBLISH TEENAGERS' WRITING

Alive for Young Teens: P.O. Box 179, St. Louis, MO 63166. If your twelve- to fifteen-year-old has written fiction, nonfiction, poetry, puzzles, riddles, or tongue-twisters, this magazine might be a good place to send it. Write for guidelines.

Byline Magazine: Student Contests, P.O. Box 130596, Edmond, OK 73013. Writing contests every month during the academic year for students eighteen years and younger. A variety of poetry and story-writing contests, some requiring a small entry fee to cover cash prizes. Send SASE for list of upcoming contests.

Guideposts Magazine: 747 Third Avenue, New York, NY 10017. *Guideposts'* Youth Writing Contest is one of the best in the nation, with over $20,000 in scholarships awarded each year for a personal experience story. Open to high school juniors and seniors. Write for contest guidelines.

Seventeen Magazine: 850 Third Avenue, New York, NY 10022. *Seventeen* publishes fiction, nonfiction, and poetry by teenagers, and has a regular column, "Free for All," open to teens. Write for guidelines and details.

REAL: 4747 Troost Avenue, Kansas City, Missouri 64110. The magazine for growing minds has a page called "Art & Soul" featuring poems and art by teenagers. Readers are also asked to make their voices heard by telling their stories, swapping opinions, and exploring issues.

The above list is only a beginning. For a more extensive list of markets for young writers, see *Market Guide for Young Writers* by Kathy Henderson, published by Writer's Digest Books. Available in libraries and bookstores, it has over 150 magazines and contests, helpful suggestions on preparing manuscripts, and profiles of young writers who have been published.

ABC Book Ideas

Animals
Colors
Spanish
Candy
Pets
Foods
Cars
Television
  shows
Nouns
Musical
  instruments
Scary things
Fantasy animals
Hobbies
Feelings

Songs
Famous People
Football Teams
Toys
Famous horses
Hurricane
  names
Companies
Military words
Foods
Holidays
Girls' names
Presidents
Verbs
Careers

Hobbies
Composers
Street names
Adjectives
Beautiful things
Books
Trees
Currency units
Sports
Computer
  language
Colleges
Countries
Boys' names
Authors

Circus
Rocks and
  Gems
Adverbs
Numbers
Dancing
Cities
Movies
Insects
Flowers
Stores
Inventors
Sounds
Flavors
Olympics